# TAKE
# TWELVE
# COOKS

# TAKE
# TWELVE
# COOKS

**THAMES MACDONALD**

A Thames Macdonald Book

First published in Great Britain in 1986
by Macdonald & Co (Publishers) Ltd
London & Sydney

A member of BPCC plc
in association with Thames Television Limited

This edition published in 1986

**British Library Cataloguing in Publication Data**
Take twelve cooks.
1. Cookery
1. Avila, Kay
641.5     TX717

ISBN 0-356-12287-5

Filmset by Flairplan Photo-typesetting Ltd

Printed and bound in Great Britain by Purnell Book Production Ltd, Paulton, near Bristol, Avon.

Editor: Catherine Rubinstein
Designer: Mike Rose
Photographers: Eric Carter, pages 50, 54, 55, 58, 66, 67, 70, 102, 103, 106-7;
Clint, pages 23, 26, 27, 30, 31, 51, 71, 74, 75, 99, 111; Clive Corless, pages 18, 19, 22, 78, 79, 98;
Bill Hugh-White, page 110, back cover; John Lee, pages 59, 62, 63; Darroch Robertson, page 46
Stylist: Dawn Lane
Home Economists: Isabelle Begg, Roz Denny, Lorna Rhodes, Polly Tyrer
Indexer: Michèle Clarke

Also available from Albert and Michel Roux:
*New Classic Cuisine*, Macdonald, 1983;
*Roux on Pâtisserie*, Macdonald, to be published in late 1986.

Macdonald & Co (Publishers) Ltd
Greater London House
Hampstead Road
London NW1 7QX

# Contents

# Introduction

Do you enjoy eating? Do you like food? If it seems odd to be asking such simple questions in the introduction to a cookery book it is because 'yes' answers are an essential prerequisite for good cooking. That is one conclusion I have come to after two series of *Take Six Cooks*. Another is that every one of the twelve cooks featured in this book is imbued with a generosity of spirit rarely found in other people. Their desire to give pleasure is unconditional: they would rather entertain than be entertained.

'The smell of cooking is the smell of life' – a Pierre Koffmann aphorism holds for them all; good cooking demands a wholehearted commitment and is therefore integral to their lives. In Albert Roux's opinion, 'You can go and see a play which you're very enchanted by and next day you can remember everybody who played in that play. I think the month after that, you remember maybe one artist – and the name of the play. A year later you remember you've seen a good play but you can't remember the name. But a fantastic meal – I think until you die you remember that.'

It is a pity to categorize our twelve cooks at all because they firmly believe that the labels given to styles of cooking are of our making, not theirs. For example, the term 'nouvelle cuisine' was first coined in the early 1970s by two journalists, Gault and Millau, who then started their guide on the strength of this development in cooking. Cooks were suddenly in or out of fashion. Pierre Koffmann believes this is bad because 'now when you go in any restaurant from Marseilles to Calais the same type of food is being served'. But fashions change and, as Raymond Blanc points out, 'if you start cooking to a fashion you are in trouble'. And even now food critics are talking about a move from nouvelle cuisine to 'French bourgeois cooking'.

In *Take Twelve Cooks*, however, a wide variety of cookery styles is represented.

**Joyce Molyneux** and **Jane Grigson** both respect the work of Elizabeth David and the link she forged between home and restaurant cooking, and this is reflected in the fish and vegetable dishes they have chosen – where tastes are generally more important than the appearance of the food.

**Peter Kromberg**, **Prue Leith** and **Richard Shepherd** all have to cater for large numbers of people, with a correspondingly wide spectrum of tastes. Their style is neither classic nor nouvelle – each has instead taken from those styles what works best for them.

**Albert and Michel Roux** and **Pierre Koffmann** (who was trained by the Roux brothers before opening his own restaurant) serve rich but light dishes, and are perhaps nearer to the classic than modern style. Their raw ingredients can be very expensive or extremely cheap, just as long as cream and butter are not compromised.

**Michael Nadell** and **John Huber**, our master pâtissiers, have both responded to the demands of nouvelle cuisine by devising lighter desserts but both believe the pendulum is swinging back to rich, classic puddings.

**Anton Mosimann, Raymond Blanc** and **Nico Ladenis**, though total individualists, do share some of the precepts of nouvelle cusine: no flour, controlled use of cream and butter, and above all exquisite presentation. Since the first series Anton has gone even further than in the recipes he has included here to develop his 'cuisine naturelle', as he calls it, which is almost free of fat and cream.

When Raymond Postgate founded the Good Food Club in 1949 (which resulted in the *Good Food Guide*), the chances of eating well in postwar Britain were minimal: 'When a landlord daringly decided to step out from his menu of overcooked meat, luncheon sausage, wrapped pies, tinned fruit and Danish Blue he added three things: Chicken Maryland, Lobster Newburg and Lemon Meringue Pie.' In 1965 he remarked, 'Gross overcooking of meat, and vegetables swimming in water are rarer phenomena than they were . . . and there is a slight – very slight – falling off of the numbers of squares of hard pastry put on to your plate next to stewed steak or stewed fruit.' It is descriptions like these that make one realize just how much the quality of food has improved in Britain in the last 30 years; indeed a Frenchman, who is also a restaurateur, recently told me that he would now stay here in London if he wanted to eat good French food.

In 1984 cooking was declared an art form by the Société des Beaux Arts, which shows clearly the new status cooks are enjoying. Raymond Blanc was thrilled – 'at last it's happened'. Pierre Koffmann, in contrast, thought it completely stupid: 'Do I call the man who does my car very well an artist?' Nico Ladenis believes the work of a cook, particularly a pâtissier, is chemistry – science certainly, but not art. Joyce Molyneux is glad that if it *is* an art, then it is an ephemeral one: 'You can eat all your mistakes so they won't live to reproach you for evermore.'

Whether a science or art, cooking should be enjoyed. In these pages you will find ideas from twelve of the best cooks in Britain. With over 120 recipes to choose from, you will certainly be able to create menus which are appropriate to any style of meal you have in mind. You can select:

hors d'oeuvres from the favourite dishes of Raymond Blanc and Prue Leith;

soups and sauces from the recipes of Nico Ladenis and Richard Shepherd;

fish recipes from the ideas of Joyce Molyneux and Anton Mosimann;

meat recipes from those of Pierre Koffmann and Albert and Michel Roux;

vegetable recipes (including main-course vegetable dishes) from Peter Kromberg and Jane Grigson;

dessert recipes supplied by Michael Nadell and John Huber.

All twelve cooks would agree that, except for the desserts, which require an exact adherence, the recipes should be regarded as a guideline, a stimulant to your own imagination. Rather than choosing a dinner-party menu and then shopping for it, it is far better to go market-shopping first to discover what is good and fresh that day, and only then consider your dishes and create your menu.

# *Raymond Blanc*
## *on*
# *Hors d'Oeuvres*

'I don't want a shrine here – I don't want a temple – I just want pure gold happiness.' So says Raymond Blanc of Le Manoir aux Quat' Saisons, a fifteenth-century Cotswold manor which has become the focus of gastronomic attention since it opened in 1984. 'Gold' happiness is particularly appropriate as over a million pounds has been put into this business venture – and, it is hoped, the achievement of Raymond Blanc's third Michelin star, the apogee for any chef. (In fact the Michelin guide, anticipating excellence at the Manoir, awarded Raymond two stars before it had even opened – creating a precedent as well as a few waves in gastronomic circles.)

Raymond's involvement in cooking began one warm summer night in his home town of Besançon, when he had a revelation. This may sound like a script for a film, but Raymond says the sight of rich and beautiful people drinking champagne in the Palais de la Bière, the clinking of glasses and the waiters in their uniforms inspired him. 'God, I knew I must enter the cuisine.' The next day he was told firmly that at nineteen he was far too old to train in the kitchen and was instead offered the humblest job in the restaurant – that of commis waiter.

But, as Raymond puts it, 'I was in – I was in the *hôtellerie*.' He came to England in 1972 to learn English and worked as a waiter at The Rose Revived, a small country hotel just outside Oxford. The film script continues . . . he married the boss's daughter, Jenny, and one night because of staff illness found himself in sole charge of the kitchen serving 70 meals.

'I'm one of those guys who couldn't have existed in the times of Escoffier because you had to have a formal training, but I did a little bit like Napoleon and took the toque and crowned myself and entered the cuisine. I know Escoffier would have turned in his grave. I am sure he has.'

In those early days Raymond was terrified and many times locked himself in the cold room convinced he couldn't cope – and he freely admits that when he employed a French *sous chef* to help him he watched him like a hawk to pick up anything he could. 'It was sweat, just pure sweat, just pure effort, just pure will, just pure dedication.' Mistakes were the clue to progress because they forced him to analyse where he had gone wrong and thus understand the actual chemistry of food. And even now when he cooks a dish he uses the opportunity to test something out – should the shredded turnip in the foie gras dish be washed to remove the starch? Likewise old and new potatoes: which give the best texture? All will be tested in pursuit of perfection.

In the last twelve years Raymond has cooked his way to stardom. Jenny has always been the business brain of their partnership and through her financial juggling of their very limited resources they found their first restaurant, tucked beneath the Oxfam headquarters in a North Oxford shopping precinct. They opened in 1977; their first Michelin star was awarded in 1979 and a second followed in 1982. And if, as it is fully expected he will, Raymond gets his third star in the next year or two, he will be the youngest chef in England ever to have done so.

Inevitably the menu at the Manoir is expensive, but all the dishes reflect Raymond's desire to excite the palate continuously. For example, a fillet of lamb will be served with crab, curry and basil; or duckling with Sauternes and a hint of ginger and white peach. 'When one mouthful tastes much like the one before, that is boring', so Raymond's dishes have four or five complementary tastes as well as textures. He admits his cooking was fussy when he began, putting far too many flavours together. He now knows when to leave well alone.

Raymond believes he was lucky to be self-taught. 'If you are under a master he will take you in hand and he will shape you the way he is – the way he would like. You get his taste and his palate – his vision of cuisine.' As it is, Raymond's palate has been described to me by other chefs as 'sheer genius – above anyone else's for actual taste and his conception of what that sauce should actually be'. Raymond believes that, although you can educate a palate to a certain extent, basically you either have a good palate or you don't. When a new chef enters his kitchen, he asks him to taste from six ramekins filled with varying strengths of salted water. 'It's amazing the differences I find – and so many chefs have this initial reflex to put salt on everything, and it's so wrong.' Delegating he finds very difficult: 'I have my own palate and guests don't want to taste somebody else's vision of cuisine.'

His vision is to provide memorable meals. And a large part of this is achieved by insisting on good ingredients; indeed Raymond attributes 80 per cent of the success of any cook to the quality of the ingredients he uses. To that end he grows up to half a dozen varieties of any one vegetable in the walled garden of the Manoir in search of the perfect taste and texture. And we as consumers must demand the same high standards. Opening a traditional French bakery in Oxford in 1980 was a lesson in that: every bakery in the vicinity looked to their own produce and started baking better bread and pâtisserie. If *we* insist, then producers – just to survive – will follow suit.

Raymond has not only survived; he has flourished. In many ways he cannot quite believe his luck. But success, though quick, has been costly: 'We give two shows a day – lunch and dinner six times a week – and every day you have this new feeling although you are absolutely broken, you are in pieces, but you have to put yourself together again.' The pressures on Raymond and Jenny Blanc are enormous. Their two young sons, Sebastian and Olivier, don't see much of their parents and Raymond and Jenny have very little spare time for each other. Both would like to let go a little, but their pursuit of perfection – and of course a third star – is relentless.

'I'm still idealistic, I still dream of perfection. I still reach for perfection knowing damn well that I'll never reach it. Sometimes there are such feelings we reach but those moments last maybe a few seconds.'

## Cèpes Farcis aux Escargots et Fumet de Vin Rouge

*Cèpes Filled with Snail and Chicken Mousse,
Served with a Red Wine Sauce*

SERVES 4

| |
|---|
| 12 medium-sized cèpes or 24 button mushrooms |
| ½ clove of garlic |
| 2 tbsp olive oil |
| 1 egg yolk whipped with 1 tbsp water |

*For the mousse*

| |
|---|
| 1 breast of chicken (120 g/4½ oz), cooked |
| 1 egg yolk |
| salt |
| 1 shallot, finely chopped |
| ½ bulb of fennel, peeled and finely diced |
| 1 tsp butter |
| 12 snails, prepared |
| pepper |
| 275 ml/9 fl oz whipping cream, chilled |
| 1 or 2 drops Pernod |

*For the breadcrumbs*

| |
|---|
| small bunch of parsley |
| 10 flaked almonds, toasted |
| ½ clove of garlic |
| 100 g/4 oz white breadcrumbs |
| 1 tbsp groundnut oil |
| 1 tsp hazelnut oil |

*For the sauce*

| |
|---|
| 4 shallots, finely chopped |
| 1 tsp butter |
| 200 ml/7 fl oz red wine |
| 100 ml/3½ fl oz concentrated veal stock |
| 1 sprig of thyme |
| ¼ clove of garlic |
| 6 tarragon leaves |

**1.** To prepare the mousse, purée the chicken breast in a blender with the egg yolk and 1 level tsp salt, then cover the bowl with a cloth and freeze for 15 minutes to cool the mixture.

**2.** Sweat the shallot and fennel in ½ tsp butter for 1 minute.

**3.** Wash the prepared snails in running cold water. Pat dry. Season and sauté for 1–2 minutes in ½ tsp hot butter. Cool. Slice 9 of the 12 snails in half lengthways (for garnish) and cut the remaining 3 into small cubes. Add these to the shallot and fennel.

**4.** Take the bowl of chicken from the freezer and mix in the chilled cream.

**5.** Add the Pernod. Taste and correct seasoning. Rub the mixture through a sieve.

**6.** Add the chopped shallot, fennel and snails to the mixture and place in the fridge.

**7.** Prepare the breadcrumbs: chop the parsley leaves finely; grind the toasted almonds; crush the garlic and purée it well.

**8.** Mix the parsley, almonds and garlic with the breadcrumbs. Add the groundnut and hazelnut oils until you get a sandy texture.

**9.** To prepare the cèpes or mushrooms, remove the stalks (reserve them for the sauce) and wipe the heads clean. Make a hollow in each head for the mousse.

**10.** Rub a frying pan with the garlic and add the olive oil. When it is really hot add the cèpes, seasoned with salt and pepper, and sauté for 1 minute only. Place upside down on a tray to cool.

**11.** Fill the cèpes with the mousse and place in the freezer for ½ hour.

**12.** To make the sauce, sweat the finely chopped shallots in butter without letting them colour, and add a quarter of the cèpe stalks or all the button mushroom stalks, chopped, and the red wine. Reduce by two-thirds.

**13.** Add the veal stock, thyme, garlic and tarragon and bring back to the boil. Reduce until you have a shiny, pouring-consistency sauce. Pass through a sieve.

**14.** Take the cèpes from the freezer, brush the mousse with the egg yolk and water mixture and then roll the cèpes in the breadcrumbs. Place on a buttered roasting tray and cook for 15 minutes at 200°C/400°F/Gas Mark 6.

**15.** Warm up the half-snails over a low heat. Place the mushrooms in the middle of a plate, pour the sauce around them and garnish with snails.

# Huîtres à la Mangue au Sabayon de Curry

*Oysters with Mango and Curry*

SERVES 4

| |
|---|
| 24 oysters from Whitstable, Colchester or Fine de Claire |
| seaweed, for presentation – or else rock salt |
| 100 g/4 oz butter |
| 3 egg yolks |
| juice of 1 lemon |
| salt |
| pepper |
| 4 tbsp double cream, whipped |
| 1 tsp curry powder |
| 3 cardamon seeds, powdered |
| 1 mango (firm but ripe) |

**1.** Scrub and wash the oysters, open them over a strainer and a fine cloth, and filter the juices through to a bowl. Take the oysters out of their shells and place them back in their juices.

**2.** Discard the top halves of the oyster shells. Wash the insides of the bottom halves and place them attractively together with the seaweed on 4 plates.

**3.** Melt 90 g/3½ oz butter in a saucepan and keep aside.

**4.** Add the egg yolks to the juices from the oysters and whisk to an emulsion – this should take about 5 minutes. Place the bowl over hot water and continue whisking until the mixture has thickened; it should be fluffy and foamy. Pour in the melted butter, whisking all the time. Add the juice of ½ lemon and season. Add the whipped cream. This is the *sabayon* sauce.

**5.** Heat the remaining butter in a small saucepan and cook the curry powder and powdered cardamon seeds for 3 minutes.

**6.** Add the oysters and cook over a high heat for about 5 seconds each side. Keep warm.

**7.** Peel the mango, cut it in half, and then dice into tiny cubes.

**8.** Warm the plates containing the seaweed and oyster shells in the oven for a few minutes, then place 1 tsp diced mango in each shell. Cover with the *sabayon* and brown lightly under the grill.

**9.** Place the curried oysters on top of the *sabayon* and squeeze a few drops of lemon juice over each oyster.

*Bon appetit!*

## Mille-Feuille de Pommes de Terre et Navets au Foie Gras avec Girolles

*Mille-Feuille of Potatoes, Turnips and Foie Gras with Wild Mushrooms*

SERVES 4

| |
| --- |
| 500 g/1 lb 2 oz potatoes |
| 120 g/4½ oz turnips |
| salt |
| pepper |
| 75 g/3 oz unsalted butter |
| 200 g/7 oz foie gras (or calf liver or chicken liver) |

*For the sauce*

| |
| --- |
| 120 g/4½ oz mushrooms, finely sliced |
| 1 tbsp sunflower or groundnut oil |
| 15 shallots |
| 15 g/½ oz butter |
| 50 ml/2 fl oz sherry vinegar |
| 50 ml/2 fl oz ruby port |
| 50 ml/2 fl oz dry Madeira |
| 150 ml/¼ pt veal stock |
| 1 sprig of thyme |
| pinch of powder of dried cèpes |
| 1 tsp old sherry (mathusalem) |
| salt |
| pepper |
| ¼ truffle (optional) |
| 1 tbsp double cream (optional) |

*For the garnish*

| |
| --- |
| 100 g/4 oz girolles (wild mushrooms – cèpes or morilles or, if necessary, button mushrooms may be used instead) |
| 10 g/¼ oz butter |
| pinch of salt |
| squeeze of lemon juice |
| 4 or 5 tarragon leaves |
| few sprigs of chervil |

**1.** Peel and finely grate the potatoes. Wash under cold running water, drain and pat dry.

**2.** Peel the turnips, grate finely and add to the potatoes. Add 3 pinches each of salt and pepper.

**3.** Melt 60 g/2½ oz of the unsalted butter, pour over the grated turnip and potato, and stir thoroughly.

**4.** Butter the bottom of a large non-stick frying pan with the remaining butter and line with a thin layer of turnip and potato. Press down with a fork, crisp gently over a medium heat for 3–4 minutes, turn and crisp again. Remove the pancake to kitchen paper to absorb excess butter. Dry in a cool oven (140°C/275°F/Gas Mark 1) for 5 minutes. Keep warm.

**5.** To make the sauce, sauté the mushrooms in very hot oil to colour them slightly.

**6.** Cut 3 shallots finely and sweat them in 1 tsp butter until well coloured. Add the sherry vinegar and heat until evaporated, then add the port, Madeira and mushrooms, and reduce by two-thirds.

**7.** Pour in the veal stock, add the thyme and powdered cèpes, and bring to the boil, skimming any impurities. Add 50 ml/2 fl oz cold water and the sherry, and pass through a fine sieve. You should have 100 ml/4 fl oz liquid. Taste and season.

**8.** Place the remaining 12 shallots in a roasting pan with the remaining butter, 6 tbsp water and a pinch of salt. Cook in the oven at 180°C/350°F/Gas Mark 4 for 20 minutes.

**9.** When the shallots are cooked and soft, reduce their juices over a strong heat until the shallots colour and caramelize.

**10.** To prepare the garnish, wipe the girolles clean and cut any large mushrooms down to the average size (if you are using dried cèpes, they should be soaked in water for 6 hours). Sauté them in a pan with the butter and salt for 1 minute only. Add the lemon juice and chopped tarragon, taste and correct seasoning. Prepare the chervil by washing and then discarding the larger stems.

**11.** Divide the foie gras into 4 pieces. Season. Heat up a thick-bottomed pan (do not add any butter – the foie gras holds plenty of fat) and smoke and sizzle the foie gras. Turn after 10 seconds and cook for another 10 seconds. Place on kitchen paper to drain excess fat and keep warm.

**12.** Cut each of the 4 slices into 4 slivers. Cut the turnip and potato pancake into 12 portions. Take 4 plates, place a piece of pancake in the middle of each plate and top with 2 slivers of foie gras, then another slice of pancake and the remaining 2 slivers of foie gras. Finish with a third layer of pancake.

**13.** Pour the sauce over the caramelized shallots and bring to the boil. If it lacks sharpness, add a dash more sherry vinegar and the truffle. If it is too sharp, add the cream. Pour it round the mille-feuille. Garnish with the girolles and sprigs of chervil.

# Pâté de Foie Gras aux Poireaux Confits

### Pâté de Foie Gras with Leeks

| MAKES 1 TERRINE |
| --- |
| 1 foie gras of 600 g/1 lb 6 oz |
| 300 ml/½ pt water |
| 300 ml/½ pt milk |
| 15 leeks |
| 100 g/4 oz salt |
| pepper |
| 1 truffle |

| *For the marinade* |
| --- |
| 1 tbsp old port |
| 1 tbsp Armagnac or Cognac |
| small pinch of salt |
| small pinch of sugar |
| small pinch of mace or nutmeg |

**1.** Remove the vein from the foie gras. Place the foie gras in a bowl containing the water and milk and leave it for 2 hours to remove all traces of blood. Dry with a cloth.

**2.** Mix the ingredients for the marinade and pour over the foie gras. Cover with cling film and leave for 12 hours in a cool place.

**3. Next day** put the foie gras into a terrine and press it down firmly. Cover with cling film. Place in a *bain marie* of hot water and put it into a preheated 110°C/225°F/Gas Mark ¼ oven for 30 minutes. Remove the terrine, cool and leave it for 24 hours in the fridge.

**4. The following day** remove the fat from the foie gras and melt it down. Slice the truffle and marinade it in warm foie gras fat for about 1 hour.

**5.** Wash the leeks and tie them into bundles of 8 and 7. Bring them to the boil in 1.5 litres/2½ pt water and 100 g/4 oz salt. Boil for 4 minutes.

**6.** Refresh the leeks under plenty of cold running water, remove string and dry off excess moisture with a cloth. Add pepper to taste.

**7.** Put the leeks with the foie gras fat and truffle in a frying pan and stir over a gentle heat for 3 minutes. Season and cool. Remove the truffle.

**8.** Cut the foie gras into slices 2 cm/¾ in thick.

**9.** Line a terrine with cling film and put in a layer of leeks, followed by a layer of truffle and a layer of foie gras. Add more leeks, then more foie gras, and finish with a layer of leeks. Cover with cling film, place a 1-kg/2-lb weight on top and leave for a day in the fridge.

**10.** Serve by slicing the pâté with a serrated knife which has been warmed in hot water.

## *Chartreuse aux Pointes d'Asperges et Poireaux à l'Infusion de Cerfeuil*

*Asparagus Mousse and Leeks with Chervil and Lemon Sauce*

| SERVES 8 |
| --- |
| 400 g/14 oz asparagus (for 250 g/9 oz spears) |
| 3 young leeks |
| salt |
| 150 g/5 oz chicken breast, raw |
| 1 egg |
| 1 egg yolk |
| 4 sprigs of chervil |
| pepper |
| 250 ml/8 fl oz milk |
| 150 ml/¼ pt whipping cream |

*For the sauce*

| |
| --- |
| 200 ml/7 fl oz vegetable stock (made from ¼ onion, white part of 1 leek, ½ stick celery, 1 small courgette, 1 tsp butter, 250 ml/8 fl oz water, small bunch of chervil, 1 parsley stalk) |
| 4 tbsp whipping cream |
| 80 g/3¼ oz cold unsalted butter, cubed |
| salt |
| pepper |
| juice of ¼ lemon |

*For the garnish*

| |
| --- |
| 10 g/¼ oz girolles (wild mushrooms) |
| 20 g/¾ oz butter |
| squeeze of lemon juice |
| 12 asparagus tips |
| 1 leek |
| salt |
| ½ truffle (optional) |
| 5 or 6 sprigs of chervil |

**1.** Cut the roots off the leeks and slice them lengthways, removing the outer two or three leaves. Cut into strips 7.5 cm/3 in long × 1 cm/½ in wide, wash them and throw into 2 litres/3½ pt boiling water with 50 g/2 oz salt for 1 minute. Remove them, reserving the cooking water, and refresh in cold water. Drain, pat dry and separate the white from the green strips.

**2.** Butter 8 ramekins and line them with overlapping leek ribbons of alternating colour radiating outwards from the centre. Part of the leeks will hang outside the ramekins.

**3.** Peel the asparagus, discarding the lower, bitter parts, and plunge the spears into the boiling salted water for 4 minutes. Refresh in cold water, drain, dry and chop roughly.

**4.** Purée the chicken, egg, egg yolk, chervil, salt and pepper in a food processor.

**5.** Purée the asparagus spears, milk and cream, add to the chicken mixture and rub through a fine sieve. Correct seasoning. Pour into the ramekins and cover with the leek strips.

**6.** Place the ramekins in a *bain marie* with hot water reaching two-thirds of the way up them and cover with buttered paper. Cook in a preheated 180°C/350°F/Gas Mark 4 oven for 20–25 minutes. After 20 minutes test to see if the mousses are firm. Keep warm in the *bain marie*.

**7.** While the mousses are cooking, prepare the vegetable stock by chopping the vegetables finely and sweating them in the butter without colouring. Add the water and herbs, and bring to the boil. Simmer for 10 minutes, then pass through a fine sieve. Discard the vegetables.

**8.** Add the cream to the stock and, over a gentle heat, whisk in the cubed, unsalted butter. Taste and season. Add the lemon juice. Keep warm.

**9.** For the garnish, sauté the girolles in half the butter for 1 minute. Add the lemon juice.

**10.** Cook the asparagus tips in boiling salted water for 4 minutes and cut in half lengthways.

**11.** Remove any coarse leaves from the leek and

chop it into small pieces. Boil in an emulsion of the rest of the butter, 6 tbsp water and a pinch of salt for 3 minutes. Add the asparagus spears to warm. Taste and add pepper.

**12.** If using a truffle, cut it into thin sticks.

**13.** Unmould the mousses into the middle of a plate and place the leeks and asparagus around them. Pour on the sauce. Scatter over the girolles and truffle sticks and top with chervil.

## Émincé d'Avocat au Crabe, Gingembre et Pamplemousse Rose

*Avocado with Crab, Ginger and Pink Grapefruit*

| SERVES 4 |
| --- |
| 2 avocados |
| 1 live crab of 675–700 g/1½ lb |
| salt |
| 30 g/1¼ oz fresh ginger root |
| 1 garden lettuce |
| 1 pink grapefruit |

| For the mayonnaise |
| --- |
| 2 egg yolks |
| ½ tsp mustard |
| salt |
| pepper |
| 300 ml/½ pt groundnut oil |
| juice of ¼ lemon |

| For the vinaigrette |
| --- |
| 100 ml/3½ fl oz groundnut oil |
| 1 tsp mustard |
| 1 tbsp white wine vinegar |
| 2 tbsp warm water |
| salt |
| pepper |

**1.** Cook the crab 3 or 4 hours before the dish is to be served: first bring to the boil 2 litres/3½ pt water with 25 g/1 oz salt. Peel the ginger root and reserve. Add the trimmings to the water – simmer for a few minutes. Clean the crab under running water, then plunge it into the boiling water and simmer for 10 minutes. Take off the heat and leave for another 10 minutes. Remove the crab from the water and cool for 1 hour.

**2.** Take all the flesh from the crab, discarding all shell and bones.

**3.** Slice the ginger root and cut it into fine sticks. Poach in boiling water for 15 minutes. Dip into cold water to refresh and keep aside.

**4.** To make the mayonnaise, mix the egg yolks with the mustard, salt and pepper, and very gradually pour in the oil. Add the lemon juice – taste and correct seasoning. Mix 2 tbsp mayonnaise with the ginger sticks and crab meat.

**5.** To make the vinaigrette, whisk the oil very slowly into the mustard. Gradually add half the vinegar and continue mixing until all the oil is absorbed. Add the remaining vinegar and warm water until the consistency is right. Season.

**6.** Wash the lettuce and pat dry. Lay 2 or 3 lettuce leaves on top of one another, then roll and shred them with a sharp knife. Toss the shredded lettuce in 2 tbsp vinaigrette.

**7.** Cut each avocado in half lengthways, peel them and slice thinly.

**8.** Remove the peel and pith from the grapefruit and cut each segment in half lengthways.

**9.** Place a mound of shredded lettuce on each plate and arrange the avocado slices around it. Spoon a little vinaigrette over them. Top with the crab salad, surrounded by the grapefruit segments.

## Tartare de Saumon Sauvage à la Croque Concombres

*Tartare of Marinated Wild Salmon with Cucumber Salad*

SERVES 8

| |
|---|
| 450 g/1 lb wild salmon fillet |
| 15 g/½ oz caster sugar |
| 15 g/½ oz table salt |
| zest of ⅛ lemon |
| 2¼ tsp chopped dill |
| ½ tsp Dijon mustard |
| 1 tsp soured cream |
| 4 turns of pepper |
| squeeze of lemon juice |

*For the cucumber salad*

| |
|---|
| 1 medium-sized cucumber |
| 15 g/½ oz table salt |
| 1 tsp white wine vinegar |
| 2 tbsp sunflower oil |
| 3 turns of pepper |

*For the garnish*

| |
|---|
| 1 tbsp chilled caviar – or lumpfish roe |
| ½ lemon |
| small bunch of dill |
| 8 tsp soured cream |

**1.** Remove the skin, stray bones and any grey parts of the flesh of the salmon.

**2.** To make the marinade, put the sugar, salt, finely cut lemon zest and 2 tsp finely chopped dill in a bowl and mix well together.

**3.** Place the salmon fillet on a piece of cling film, cover with the marinade and wrap into a parcel. Put in the bottom of the fridge for 12 hours.

**4.** After 12 hours scrape off the marinade and wash off any salt residue under cold running water. Pat dry.

**5.** Cut the salmon flesh into 5-mm/¼-in cubes.

**6.** In a separate bowl, carefully mix the Dijon mustard, soured cream, pepper, lemon juice and remaining dill, then add the cubed salmon and stir well. Taste and correct seasoning. Keep in a cool place for 1 hour.

**7.** To make the cucumber salad, peel the cucumber and cut it in half lengthways. Remove the seeds with a teaspoon. Cut the two halves into very fine slices. Put them in a colander, sprinkle with salt and leave for ½ hour.

**8.** Wash the cucumber slices under running water, pat them dry and put them in a bowl with the white wine vinegar, sunflower oil and pepper. Mix thoroughly.

**9.** Prepare the garnishes: chill the caviar; remove the skin and pith from the lemon and then cut the flesh into tiny triangles; cut the leaves of dill off the main stem to form a frill.

**10.** For each person, place a 6-cm/2½-in diameter pastry cutter in the centre of a plate and fill it four-fifths full with salmon. Press down gently with a spoon.

**11.** Top the salmon with 1 tsp soured cream and smooth the top with a palette knife. Ease off the pastry cutter.

**12.** Arrange the cucumber around the salmon, overlapping the slices. Garnish the soured cream top with 6 triangles of lemon and put a little caviar in the middle. Arrange the frill of dill leaves round the edge of the tartare.

# Prue Leith
## on
# Hors d'Oeuvres

'I know fifty cooks who are better than me. But I know good food when I see it.' Prue Leith's view of herself explains how she has made such a successful career out of food. She is realistic about her own talents as a cook and also extremely canny when it comes to the business of food, the needs of her customers, and the needs of her readers, too.

She did not always demonstrate such talent. She knew nothing about cooking and had even less interest in food during her days in South Africa, where she lived until she was nineteen.

Having failed miserably to get a degree in South Africa (one of her few failures), she went to Paris as an au pair to learn French. But it was the care the *maman* took with the cooking that impressed Prue more than the language. 'I remember counting the number of ingredients that went into something as simple as stuffed pancakes. Seventeen. I could hardly believe it.' Needless to add, she never let Prue cook anything: 'The very fact that I spoke English meant I must totally ruin the food.'

On returning to London from Paris, she managed to bluff her way on to an advanced Cordon Bleu course. 'It's very sound cooking. You can learn a lot.'

Prue tested her theories by cooking directors' lunches. Her Bible was – and it still is a constant reference – a pink and faded Constance Spry cookbook. 'It's a sort of domestic equivalent to Mrs Beeton. I religiously cooked my way from cover to cover – 1100 pages crammed with information. My directors were the guinea pigs. I remember getting to the suet pudding chapter in the middle of July and those poor chaps just had to eat their way through it with me.' Ever the entrepreneur, Prue spent her evenings doing private dinners and cocktail parties. 'A terrifying experience. There's no one to blame but yourself – but the beauty of it is you really don't need any capital at all.'

Public transport, on which Prue used to ferry her food, was eventually replaced by a minivan: now there is a fleet and Leith's Good Food serves 3000 main courses a month and canapés for 1100 people. Three mouthfuls a head – or four if the guests are hungry – is the cocktail party allowance; such precision is one reason for the success of Prue's catering empire.

Economy and efficiency have been learned the hard way. Within six months of opening Leith's Restaurant in 1969 in Notting Hill Gate, Prue lost money hand over fist: 'I didn't know

**Raymond Blanc** *Mille-Feuille de Pommes de Terre et Navets au Foie Gras avec Girolles (page 12)*

**Raymond Blanc** *Chartreuse aux Pointes d'Asperges et Poireaux à l'Infusion de Cerfeuil (page 14)*

anything about accounts and control and it never occurred to me that everybody was robbing me blind.' She called in Albert Roux of Le Gavroche to see where on earth she was going wrong. Instead of looking at her books, Albert first sat by the dustbin in the kitchen and made a mental note of what was being put into it. 'You're throwing good food away' was his verdict. The cooks were discarding ingredients Albert would have directed to other parts of the kitchen – if only to the stock pot.

Leith's School of Food and Wine was opened in 1975. 'We teach very much in the Cordon Bleu manner – each student cooks everything.' But Prue almost despairs of students who breeze in claiming that they are so creative that they never need to look at a recipe: 'A little bit of this and a bit of that . . . it's nonsense. To know what goes with what you've got to understand the basics, and so often people don't.' Prue is very keen that students know their wines as well as their cooking basics. 'I think far too many cooks learn to cook without any knowledge of wine at all and that's a bit crazy.' No one can get a Leith certificate without a wine certificate.

Surely, sometimes compromises must be necessary both in the restaurant and in the catering services? 'Not over ingredients – but we do adapt our methods sometimes.' In the restaurant they pre-cook vegetables – a cardinal sin to many cooks, but according to Prue 'they are boiled so fast that they lose no colour, very few vitamins, and they're cooled so fast that they don't go grey and mushy'. When needed they are put into individual dishes with a little butter and microwaved. Prue also freezes soufflé mixture, a trick she got from the Café Royal. Orange and Lemon St Clement's Soufflé on the menu at Leith's is prepared beforehand and frozen in individual ramekins. When needed they can be heated in seventeen minutes in a soufflé oven 'and they are absolutely perfect'.

At the farm, an Elizabethan manor house at Chastleton Glebe, Prue has developed the kitchen garden which now supplies the restaurant and the school with fresh produce. Peas, beans, potatoes are picked when they are still tiny; raspberries, blackcurrants – every kind of fruit and herb is there. Even Chinese gooseberries are coated with sugar and served as petits fours. A sense of business prevails even here in the garden. Produce must be cost-effective: Prue tried to rear her own ducks, but she found other people could do it far more cheaply.

Since her marriage to South African writer Rayne Kruger, who now shares the burden of Leith business, and the advent of her two children, Prue considers she has slowed down, but she still manages to cram a quart into a pint pot, dividing her time between home and London. Home is the place to write her books, her weekly column for the *Guardian*. London is the place for meetings – not just to do with the Leith empire, but British Rail board meetings too, of which she has been a member for four years. Prue was once described by Sir Peter Parker as the lady who uncurled the British Rail sandwich. She believes that her woman's eye for detail makes her useful to British Rail, who are well aware that she makes money from her food.

Prue does not hide the fact that she gets ideas from other people all the time. She is not slow to praise those she admires. Constance Spry may have been her early mentor but Elizabeth David also inspired her from the start. Jane Grigson is another cook and writer high in her regard. Perhaps it is because both Jane and Elizabeth David enjoy food without being obsessive that Prue feels at home with them: 'There are definitely two people in me; one is the gastronome who wants food to be absolutely perfect and the other is impatient with people who go on about food eternally. I love eating it but pretentious conversation about food irritates me.'

# Avocado with Redcurrant Vinaigrette

| 1 avocado per person, peeled and sliced |
| salad oil |
| lemon juice |
| fresh redcurrants |
| sugar |
| salt |
| pepper |

**1.** In a blender, combine 4 parts oil and 1 part lemon juice with sufficient redcurrants to colour the sauce pink, thicken it and give a good sharp flavour.

**2.** Add sugar, salt and pepper to taste.

**3.** Pour 2 or 3 tbsp of the sauce on to each plate and arrange the sliced avocado on top.

# Guacamole

SERVES 4–6

| 4 large ripe avocados, peeled and mashed or chopped |
| 1 small onion, minced or chopped |
| juice of 1 lemon |
| 2 tbsp olive oil |
| 2 cloves of garlic, crushed |
| 2 tbsp chopped fresh tomato |
| small pinch of coriander or 1 tsp fresh coriander leaves, chopped |

**1.** Mix all the prepared ingredients, liquids and herbs together.

**2.** Spoon into a serving dish, and serve with hot toast.

# Lasagne Ring Mould

SERVES 4–6

| 450 g/1 lb lasagne |
| butter for frying |
| 4 rashers rindless streaky bacon, chopped |
| 1 large onion, finely chopped |
| 100 g/4 oz Cheddar cheese, grated |
| 2 whole eggs |
| 2 egg yolks |
| 300 ml/½ pt cream |
| 300 ml/½ pt milk |
| salt |
| pepper |

**1.** Cook the lasagne according to the packet instructions, then rinse well under hot running water to remove the surface starch.

**2.** Line a buttered ring mould (900-ml/1½-pt size) with overlapping pieces of pasta.

**3.** Fry the bacon until just brown. Add the onion and cook until soft. If the pan becomes too dry add some extra butter.

**4.** Mix the cheese, eggs, egg yolks, cream and milk.

**5.** Add the contents from the frying pan. Check the seasoning.

**6.** Carefully pour the mixture into the mould. Stand the mould in a roasting tin two-thirds full of hot water and bake in the oven at 190°C/ 375°F/Gas Mark 5 for 45 minutes, or until the custard has just set.

**7.** Place a heated serving dish upside down over the mould. Invert the mould and plate and give a sharp shake to dislodge the lasagne on to the plate.

**Raymond Blanc** *Huîtres à la Mangue au Sabayon de Curry (page 11)*

**Prue Leith** *Avocado with Redcurrant Vinaigrette (page 21)*

## Vegetable and Fish Terrine

SERVES 6

| |
|---|
| 350 g/12 oz whiting, skinned and boned |
| 350 g/12 oz salmon, skinned and boned |
| 2 large egg whites |
| 450 ml/¾ pt double cream, chilled |
| salt |
| pepper |
| pinch of nutmeg |
| 6 long thin French beans, cooked |
| 6 long thin sticks of carrot, cooked |

*For the sauce*

| |
|---|
| 300 ml/½ pt strong fish stock made from the bones, heads, skin, etc |
| 100 g/4 oz butter, chilled and cut into chunks |
| 15 g/½ oz flour |
| salt |
| pepper |
| lemon juice |
| 2 tbsp cream |

1. Put the whiting and salmon in a food processor, or mince it twice, or rub through a hair sieve – it must be absolutely smooth.
2. Beat in the egg whites.
3. Chill well, then mix in the cream by hand and not over-vigorously – you should have a sloppy, just stable, mixture. Season with salt, pepper and a little nutmeg.
4. Line a loaf tin with buttered foil. Spoon one-third of the mixture into the tin, then arrange a line of cooked carrots and one of beans, end to end and slightly apart from each other, down the tin. Add more filling, then two more rows of vegetables. Finally smooth in the rest of the filling, and cover with buttered foil.
5. Stand the tin in a roasting tin of boiling water and cook gently, with the water barely simmer-

ing, in the oven at 180°C/350°F/Gas Mark 5 for 40–50 minutes or until the terrine is set.
6. Allow to cool completely, then refrigerate.
7. To serve, place a slice of terrine on a warm plate. Warm gently, covered in polywrap in a microwave oven, or covered with foil in a cool oven (140°C/275°F/Gas Mark 1).
8. To make the sauce, melt 15 g/½ oz of the butter, stir in the flour, and then the stock. Stir until boiling.
9. Keep just boiling while you beat in the chilled butter over a moderate heat, one piece at a time.
10. Add seasoning and a little lemon juice, and finally the cream. Pour around the terrine just before serving.

## Trout with Poppyseed Dressing

SERVES 4–6

| |
|---|
| 1 whole pink trout |
| 1 tbsp poppyseeds |
| ground black pepper |
| sea salt |
| 3 tbsp olive oil |
| juice of 1 lime |

1. Slice the very fresh raw pink trout (or farmed salmon or sea trout) as you would smoked salmon.
2. Spread carefully over dinner plates so the pieces touch but do not overlap. Cover with polywrap and chill.
3. Just before serving, sprinkle with poppyseeds, coarsely ground black pepper, sea salt, olive oil and a little fresh lime juice.

## Scallops with Saffron Sauce, on Mâche

| SERVES 4 |
| --- |
| 16 fresh scallops |
| 2 handfuls fresh *mâche* (lamb's lettuce) |
| olive oil |
| sea salt |
| pepper |
| pinch of saffron threads |
| 1 tbsp white wine |
| 25 g/1 oz butter |
| 2 shallots, chopped |
| 300 ml/½ pt very fresh double cream |

**1.** Place a well-washed salad of *mâche* on individual cold plates. Just before serving, sprinkle lightly with olive oil, sea salt and pepper.
**2.** Put the saffron in a small pan with the white wine and 1 tbsp water. Bring to the boil and set aside to infuse.
**3.** Remove any black particles and the fibrous muscle (from opposite the orange 'coral') from the scallops. Rinse and dry them.
**4.** Heat the butter in a heavy sauté pan and gently cook the shallots in it.
**5.** When they are soft and transparent-looking, add the scallops and turn up the heat to cook them, for about 2 minutes per side – just enough for them to stiffen without becoming shrunken or tough. When just firm and no longer glassy, slide them back on to a plate to keep warm for a few seconds.
**6.** Add the strained saffron juice and boil rapidly until there is only 1 tsp or so left.
**7.** Then add the cream and boil very fast until the sauce is reduced to a slightly thickened cream.
**8.** Slide 4 scallops on to each bed of lettuce and divide the sauce between them. Serve at once.

## Pumpkin and Tarragon Soup

| SERVES 4–6 |
| --- |
| 450 g/1 lb pumpkin |
| 1 large onion, sliced |
| 50 g/2 oz butter, for frying |
| 450 g/1 lb potatoes, peeled and sliced |
| 1 small clove of garlic, crushed |
| 600 ml/1 pt good chicken stock |
| salt |
| pepper |
| 4 sprigs of tarragon, leaves only |
| 600 ml/1 pt creamy milk |
| 3 tbsp cream |

**1.** Peel the pumpkin, discarding the seeds, and cut into chunks.
**2.** Slowly cook the onion in the butter until soft and transparent.
**3.** Add the pumpkin, potatoes and garlic. Cover the pan and cook until the vegetables are soft (15–20 minutes) over a moderate flame.
**4.** Add the stock, salt and pepper and half the tarragon leaves, and bring to the boil. Liquidize.
**5.** Add the milk and reheat the liquid without letting it boil.
**6.** Add the remaining tarragon and stir in the cream, again without letting it boil. Serve.

**Prue Leith** *Stilton Mousse with Candied Pear and Mint Sauce (page 28)*

**Prue Leith** *Trout with Poppyseed Dressing (page 24)*

## Stilton Mousse with Candied Pear and Mint Sauce

SERVES 6

*For the mousse*

175 g/6 oz creamy Stilton, skinned

150 ml/¼ pt double cream, whipped

*For the pears*

6 very small pears

300 ml/½ pt water

225 g/8 oz sugar

6 sprigs of mint

*For the sauce*

3 eggs

1 tbsp lemon juice

2 tsp wine vinegar

1 tbsp chopped fresh mint

2 tbsp double cream

**1.** Mix the Stilton and whipped cream together and form into 6 neat spoonfuls, one to each plate. Chill.
**2.** Peel and core the pears. Boil the water and sugar together to make a syrup and cook the pears in the syrup until glassy and tender. Cool.
**3.** Put 1 tbsp pear syrup, the eggs, lemon juice and vinegar in a bowl and set it over a saucepan of simmering water. Whisk the egg mixture steadily over the heat until it is thick enough to leave a ribbon trail when the whisk is lifted. Allow to cool, whisking frequently.
**4.** Once cold, add the mint and cream.

**5.** Place a pear on each plate. Slice it through – from its wide end to its stalk, without quite separating the slices from the narrow end. Fan them out slightly. Put a mint sprig at the stalk end of each pear.
**6.** Spoon the mint sauce round each pear and serve the dish with fingers of toast.

## Mushroom and Coriander Pâté or Dip

SERVES 4–6

450 g/1 lb mushrooms

50 g/2 oz butter

1 small clove of garlic, crushed

1 tsp coriander berries, crushed

1 small carton soured cream

salt

freshly ground black pepper

**1.** Slice the mushrooms and fry them in the butter with the garlic and coriander until they are just cooked.
**2.** Liquidize with the pan juices.
**3.** When cool, add the soured cream and season with salt and pepper.
**4.** Chill before serving with fingers of toast or hot wholemeal rolls.

# Twice-Baked Soufflé

| SERVES 8 |
| --- |
| 450 ml/¾ pt milk |
| slice of onion |
| pinch of nutmeg |
| 75 g/3 oz butter |
| 75 g/3 oz flour |
| pinch of dry English mustard |
| 250 g/9 oz strong Cheddar, grated |
| 6 eggs, separated |
| salt |
| pepper |
| 450 ml/¾ pt single cream or white sauce |

1. Butter the insides of 8 teacups.
2. Heat the milk slowly with the onion and nutmeg. Remove the onion.
3. Melt the butter, and stir in the flour and the mustard. Add the milk, off the heat, whisking until the mixture is smooth.
4. Return to the heat and bring to the boil, stirring all the time.
5. When thickened, remove from the heat, and add 225 g/8 oz of the cheese. Stir in the egg yolks and check the seasoning.
6. Whisk the egg whites until stiff and fold into the cheese mixture.
7. Fill the teacups two-thirds full with the mixture. Stand them in a roasting tin of boiling water and bake at 190°C/375°F/Gas Mark 5 for 15–20 minutes or until set.
8. Allow to sink and cool, then loosen the soufflés and turn them out into a buttered ovenproof dish.
9. Heat the oven to 230°C/450°F/Gas Mark 8. Sprinkle the remaining cheese over the top of the soufflés and coat them with the cream, seasoned with salt and pepper. Bake for 15 minutes or until risen and brown.

# Tudor Salad

| SERVES 6 |
| --- |
| 350 g/12 oz duck or poultry livers, cleaned |
| 100 g/4 oz mange-tout |
| 100 g/4 oz tiny French beans |
| 2 sorrel leaves |
| 6 nasturtium flowers |
| 12 borage flowers |
| few sprigs of chervil |
| 2 shallots, chopped |
| oil for frying |

| *For the dressing* |
| --- |
| 4 tbsp light olive oil |
| 2 tsp red wine vinegar |
| 2 tsp lemon juice |
| ½ tsp English mustard |
| sea salt |
| black pepper |

1. Cook the mange-tout and beans whole in separate pans of boiling salted water. Drain, cool under the cold tap, and pat dry. Top and tail them and put together in a bowl.
2. Shred the sorrel leaves as finely as possible and add them to the peas and beans.
3. Mix all the dressing ingredients together.
4. Toss the salad in the dressing, then place on six wide-bordered plates.
5. Arrange the petals of the nasturtium flowers, and the whole borage flowrs, alternately with tiny sprigs of chervil, to make a decorative border around the plate.
6. Just before serving, cook the shallots slowly in a little oil until soft and cooked.
7. Then turn the heat to moderate and add the livers. Cook for about 3 minutes each side, or until they are just firm but still pink in the middle.
8. Add the hot livers and the juice from the pan to the salad, and serve at once.

**Nico Ladenis** *Top, Coulis of Tomatoes (page 36) served with brill with vermouth fish sauce; bottom, Fumée de Cèpes (page 37) served with duck.*

**Nico Ladenis** *Rosemary Butter Sauce (page 37) served with red mullet*

# Nico Ladenis
## on
# Soups & Sauces

When Nico Ladenis graduated from Hull University in 1958 with an Economics degree his career prospects seemed rosy, but vocational tests later revealed that he was 'non-conformist, incapable of being managed and unemployable' – a conclusion Nico had long since privately reached. The only solution was to work for himself. But what did he really like doing? That question was not answered until some time later during a year off in the South of France, where Nico and his wife Dinah literally ate their savings in the best restaurants they could find. Nico couldn't cook but that didn't matter – he could learn; and when he got back to England he combined his memories of those good French meals with two books – *French Provincial Cookery* by Elizabeth David and *The Masterpieces of French Cuisine* by France Amentegui – and taught himself to cook. When most chefs would have fifteen or twenty years' experience behind them, Nico at the age of 35 was just beginning. But he certainly looked the part – 5′ 10″ and 16 stone, with dark,

typically Mediterranean looks.

The first, and Nico believes the best, meal he ever cooked was before he and Dinah had opened their first restaurant. It was a Poulet au Vin Jura, using a £15 bottle of wine from the Jura, 'the height of extravagance'. Ironically, it is a dish Nico wants to put on his menu at Chez Nico in Reading, which opened in September 1985. He opened his first Chez Nico in Lordship Lane, Dulwich – and, as the *Good Food Guide* commented in 1975, 'Lordship Lane is not an aristocratic address'. Five years later, however, they were saying that 'over the past five years this has probably been the best and certainly the most imaginative chef/patron restaurant in London'.

Nico was a colourful character to enter the London restaurant world. He refused to show a menu in his window, telling people instead that they could take him or leave him – 'a very high-handed attitude but I had nothing to lose'. And people took notice of him, if sometimes in fear. For Nico Ladenis is 'totally evangelical' in his belief that the customer is not always right. 'My view is that if a customer is demonstrably wrong, is openly rude, you do not offer them a glass of champagne. If they steal cutlery, I call the police.' People who have asked for salt and pepper rarely come back, and if their evening was ruined, so too was Nico's. But his tenacity has paid off. In 1979 he moved further into London to Chez Nico Battersea – again not a likely address for a restaurant which gained its first star within nine months of opening and its second star in 1984. But within sight of Battersea Power Station Nico has cooked some of the best food in England.

His style of cooking has been described as 'assimilating the ideas of nouvelle cuisine while rejecting its irrelevant gestures'. Nico calls it 'old-velle' or 'classic French served in a modern way'. In spirit he compares himself to Roger Vergé at the Moulin de Mougins near Cannes, a non-conformist among French three-star chefs. Vergé is a man who prefers strong-flavoured food, and is completely self-taught, flair replacing any formal training. Indeed the best dish Nico has ever eaten was cooked by Vergé – Salade Moulin de Mougins – fresh uncooked truffles, langouste, artichokes, beans and oranges served with a butter sauce with truffle juices. But if Nico identifies with Vergé, he believes that the biggest influence on food in the 1970s was Michel Guérard with his book *Cuisine Gourmande*; that it was he who really projected the philosophy of nouvelle cusine. Its publication coincided with Nico's first attempts at cooking 'so I took a short cut. I didn't learn how to do a sauce béchamel or a sauce espagnole. I went straight to reductions,' thus avoiding the use of flour, finishing the sauce instead mostly with cream – though in brown sauces extra butter gives the right thickness and gloss.

If Nico favours one task in the kitchen it is making sauces, which makes it difficult to forget the three people who came into the restaurant and asked for a plain salad and steamed sole. When it arrived, one of the party asked the waitress for a sauceboat and then took a bottle out of his pocket and poured it in. It was Texas chilli sauce. What made it worse was that they thought the meal was wonderful. 'They besmirched my restaurant,' so Nico chased them up the street to give their money back, but they disappeared into the night. But Nico concedes he may be mellowing as he gets older because, arguing against himself, he does have the utmost respect for three-star restaurants which accommodate customers' idiosyncracies.

He won't relax until he gets his third star: 'In life you've got to do something. I just want to make a mark in life – and I want to prove one or two points to people as well – like you don't have to have a classical French training to reach that level. If I ever get three stars I will be the only non-French three-star in England and for me that's important.'

The new Chez Nico at Shinfield, near Reading, really is destined for three stars. It is an old Victorian vicarage which has been completely redesigned at a cost of £500,000. Nico is no longer his own master because he is now answerable to shareholders, which made the move a difficult one for him and Dinah. Luckily, they have made many firm friends, and customers have proved to be loyal. Some dishes have survived the move too – like Fish Soup, Consommé and Terrine de Foie Gras; Dinah and Nico were reluctant to tempt fate by changing things too much. The move has given Nico more room for his two passions: food and Alsatians. After their cramped home in Chelsea, the dogs are thriving in the country; after being released from his cramped kitchen in Battersea, Nico now has room for his third star. His immediate challenge, however, is to convert the home counties to Chez Nico tastes.

## Avgolemono

SERVES 8

| |
|---|
| 2 tbsp basmati rice |
| 6 egg yolks |
| 1 litre/1¾ pt chicken stock (see recipe p 41) |
| 2 tbsp double cream (well beaten but not stiff) |
| salt |
| lemon juice to taste |
| pepper |

*For the garnish*

| |
|---|
| tiny croutons |
| goose fat |

1. Cook the basmati rice in boiling water, then drain it and leave on one side to dry.
2. Brush the croutons for the garnish with goose fat and bake in a 220–230°C/425–450°F/ Gas Mark 7–8 oven for 6 minutes.
3. Whisk the egg yolks in a glass bowl until thick.
4. Heat the chicken stock in a small casserole dish.
5. When the chicken stock is hot, add the rice and egg yolks in a steady thin stream, stirring carefully all the time. Regulate the heat to stop the egg scrambling in the liquid.
6. Add the cream and keep on stirring over the heat until the eggs start to thicken slightly and the cream gives a fluffy, frothy top to the soup. (This is a difficult soup because it can curdle easily, but you must give it sufficient heat for the eggs to cook and to thicken the soup.)
7. Adjust the seasoning, add as much lemon juice as your taste requires and keep on stirring.
8. Spoon into individual soup bowls. Grind some black peppercorns over the soup and decorate with the croutons.

## Consommé de Champignons au Madère Aromatisé aux Feuilles de Coriandre

*Mushroom Consommé with Madeira, Falvoured with Coriander Leaves*

SERVES 6–8

| |
|---|
| 450 g/1 lb button mushrooms |
| 40 g/1½ oz fresh foie gras |
| 100 g/4 oz onion, very finely chopped |
| 1 large tbsp tomato purée |
| 2.25 litres/4 pt chicken stock (see recipe p 41) into which some tomatoes have been cooked |
| 85 ml/3 fl oz Madeira |
| 3 egg whites |
| salt |
| coriander leaves |

1. Mince the mushrooms in a food processor.
2. Melt the foie gras in a large saucepan, add the onion and sauté until transparent.
3. Add the tomato purée, chicken stock and mushrooms, and cook for 1 hour. Just before removing from the heat, add 50 ml/2 fl oz Madeira.
4. Force the liquid and mushrooms through a fine sieve.
5. Allow the liquid to cool and then beat it into the egg whites with a whisk in a clean saucepan. Continue beating until all liquid is added and the egg whites have been well amalgamated.
6. Place the soup on a very low heat, bring to simmering-point and cook for ½–¾ hour to clarify.
7. Add more Madeira and salt to taste.
8. Pour the liquid through two or three layers of muslin or a jelly bag. Serve in bowls with coriander leaves floating on top.

## Fish Soup

SERVES 6–8

| |
|---|
| 1 kg/2¼ lb mixed Mediterranean fish (red mullet, grondin, rascasse, weaverfish, conger eel, crushed lobster or langoustine shells) |
| 65 ml/2½ fl oz good olive oil |
| 25 ml/1 fl oz clarified butter |
| a *mirepoix* of 75 g/3 oz each of fennel, carrots, onions, leeks and celery, diced |
| 25 g/1 oz chopped shallot |
| 6 cloves of garlic |
| 300 ml/½ pt white wine |
| 120 ml/4 fl oz red wine |
| 120 ml/4 fl oz ruby port |
| 50 ml/2 fl oz brandy |
| 225-g/8-oz tin Italian tomatoes |
| 150-g/5-oz tin tomato purée |
| strip of orange peel |
| 1 tbsp wild savory |
| 1 tbsp crushed fennel seed |
| ½ tbsp star anise |
| 1 tbsp tarragon |
| 1 tbsp thyme |
| 1 tbsp parsley |
| 2 bay leaves |
| 1 tbsp mixed Provençale herbs |
| 9 leaves fresh basil |
| 50 ml/2 fl oz pastis |
| 1 tbsp saffron |
| salt |
| cayenne pepper |

**1.** Heat the olive oil and clarified butter in a large pan. Sauté the *mirepoix*, shallot and 3 cloves of garlic, halved, gently until golden.
**2.** Deglaze by stirring in the white wine.
**3.** Add the red wine, port and brandy. Cook for a while to allow the alcohol to evaporate, then add the tomatoes, tomato purée, orange peel, flavourings, 3 basil leaves and other herbs.

**4.** Cut the fish into small pieces and add to the pan. Cook for 5 minutes over moderate heat and then add water almost to the top of the pan.
**5.** Simmer the soup for 1½ hours, uncovered.
**6.** After 1 hour add the remaining basil, the pastis and the remaining garlic, finely sliced; 5 minutes before the end, add the saffron.
**7.** Remove any large bones, liquidize the soup in batches in a blender and pass it through a drum sieve, squeezing out all the liquid.
**8.** Sieve the soup a second time into a clean pot.
**9.** Reheat and season with salt and just enough cayenne pepper to feel the heat on the tongue.

## Crème de Girolles

*Girolle Cream*

'My favourite – and simplest – sauce.'

SERVES 4–6

| |
|---|
| 225 g/8 oz dried girolles (wild mushrooms) |
| 1 dessertsp chopped shallot |
| 1 tbsp chives |
| 900 ml/1½ pt chicken stock |
| 900 ml/1½ pt double cream |

**1.** Place the girolles, shallot, chives and chicken stock into a small casserole and bring to the boil. Simmer for 1 hour.
**2.** Pass through muslin into a glass bowl and allow all the sediment from the girolles to settle.
**3.** After 1 hour carefully tip the liquid into a saucepan, discarding the sediment. Add the double cream and cook until you get a slightly syrupy consistency and the sauce has acquired an 'absolutely heavenly' flavour.

Serve with any white meat – such as chicken, veal, pork, sweetbreads or rabbit.

## Cooked Vinaigrette

This is the basis of all salad dressings and some sauces at Chez Nico.

| |
|---|
| 1.5 litres/2½ pt good olive oil |
| 150 ml/¼ pt white wine |
| 85 ml/3 fl oz white wine vinegar |
| 75 g/3 oz carrots, chopped |
| 75 g/3 oz celery, chopped |
| 75 g/3 oz onions, chopped |
| 50 g/2 oz leeks, chopped |
| 50 g/2 oz fennel, chopped |
| 50 g/2 oz red pepper, chopped |
| sliver of orange peel |
| 12 black peppercorns |
| 1 bay leaf |
| 2 sprigs of rosemary |
| 2 sprigs of thyme |
| 2 sprigs of parsley |
| 2 sprigs of tarragon |
| 1 tbsp sugar |

**1.** Mix the olive oil, wine and vinegar in a cast-iron enamelled pot.
**2.** Add the vegetables and other ingredients and cook for ¾ hour on an extremely low heat.
**3.** Remove from the heat, cover with a cloth and allow to infuse for another hour.
**4.** Strain the mixture through muslin, cool and then store in the fridge, preferably in bottles with a squirt top to aid sprinkling – or else in screw-top bottles.

**For salads** use a combination of 2 parts cooked vinaigrette to 1 part hazelnut oil and a drop of lemon juice.

**For tomato coulis** see following recipe.

**For an orange sauce** (to serve with fillets of Dover sole) reduce some orange juice, add the cooked vinaigrette and thicken with butter.

## Coulis of Tomatoes

SERVES 4–6

| |
|---|
| 900 g/2 lb very red tomatoes, skinned and de-seeded |
| 2–3 large bunches of basil |
| 2–3 large bunches of tarragon |
| 1 tbsp sugar |
| 1 tsp cayenne pepper |
| 250 ml/8 fl oz pure olive oil |
| 250 ml/8 fl oz cooked vinaigrette (see previous recipe) |

**1.** Place the tomatoes, chopped, in a large bowl.
**2.** Chop the basil and tarragon and add to the tomatoes, along with the sugar and a little cayenne pepper. Mix well together.
**3.** Add the olive oil and the cooked vinaigrette and stir together.
**4.** Cover the mixture with a cloth and leave to one side to infuse for 4 hours.
**5.** Then pass the mixture through a *mouli-légumes* or blender.
**6.** Line a sieve with muslin, pour in the pulp and drain off all the thin, insipid tomato water.
**7.** The pulp that remains in the sieve is the tomato coulis. Adjust seasoning to taste.

This sauce may be served cold with marinated raw salmon or smoked salmon, or hot with any fish – for example brill. To serve hot, warm the coulis very carefully, whisking it, to avoid separation of the mixture.

# Rosemary Butter Sauce

| SERVES 4–6 |
| --- |
| 2 bunches of rosemary, leaves only |
| 16 crushed black peppercorns |
| 100 g/4 oz garlic, chopped |
| 400 g/14 oz butter |
| 225 g/8 oz shallots, chopped |
| 250 ml/8 fl oz white wine |
| 175 ml/6 fl oz white wine vinegar |
| 85 ml/3 fl oz white fish stock (see recipe p 41) |
| 3–4 tbsp double cream |

**1.** Sauté the rosemary, crushed peppercorns and garlic in 25 g/1 oz butter.
**2.** Add the shallots, then the white wine and white wine vinegar, and reduce by boiling until the sauce coats the back of a spoon.
**3.** Add the white fish stock and cook until reduced to practically a glaze.
**4.** Add the double cream. Slice the rest of the butter and add a little at a time. Pass through a sieve.
**5.** If the sauce is too thick, it may be thinned a little by adding milk (it should be of a light, pouring consistency).

Serve with grilled red mullet.

# Fumée de Cèpes

| SERVES 4–6 |
| --- |
| 250 g/9 oz dried cèpes |
| 4 or 5 ripe tomatoes, de-seeded |
| a *mirepoix* of 50 g/2 oz carrots, 50 g/2 oz shallots and 25 g/1 oz each of onion, celery and leek, diced |
| ½ clove of garlic, finely sliced |
| 1 bay leaf |
| 1 sprig of thyme |
| 2 litres/3½ pt veal stock (see recipe p 41) |
| 120 ml/4 fl oz ruby port |
| 50 ml/2 fl oz Cognac |
| 10 g/¼ oz butter |

**1.** Mix the tomatoes, *mirepoix*, garlic, herbs and dried cèpes in an ovenproof dish and brown them in the oven for 15 minutes at 200°C/400°F/ Gas Mark 6.
**2.** Place these vegetables and herbs in a large saucepan, add the veal stock, port and some of the Cognac, bring to the boil and simmer slowly for 2 hours.
**3.** Strain twice through muslin and skim off any fat.
**4.** To make the final sauce, reduce 200 ml/7 fl oz of the mixture by half in a copper saucepan so that it coats the back of a spoon, sprinkle in a little more Cognac and thicken with butter.

This sauce goes well with duck, grouse or pheasant.

## Purée d'Ail Doux

### Garlic Purée

SERVES 4–6

| |
|---|
| 13 cloves of garlic |
| a *mirepoix* of 75 g/3 oz each of carrots, onions, celery and leeks, diced |
| 2 sprigs of rosemary |
| 2 sprigs of thyme |
| 1 sprig of tarragon |
| 2 sprigs of parsley |
| 150 ml/¼ pt ruby port |
| 50 ml/2 fl oz Cognac |
| 600 ml/1 pt good brown veal stock (see recipe p 41) |
| 2 tbsp clarified butter |
| 175 ml/6 fl oz double cream |
| 175 ml/6 fl oz chicken stock |

**1.** Simmer 1 clove of garlic, the *mirepoix*, rosemary, thyme, tarragon and parsley with the port and Cognac in the veal stock until it has reduced to about 85 ml/3 fl oz, then pass it through muslin. (Its consistency should be thick, like a *glace de viande*.)

**2.** Clean the 12 remaining cloves of garlic and mix them with the clarified butter. Wrap in foil and roast on a baking tray in the oven at 200°C/400°F/Gas Mark 6 for 45 minutes until the garlic forms a purée.

**3.** Cook the cream with the chicken stock until it thickens slightly and add this mixture to the garlic and the reduced veal stock.

**4.** Pass the mixture through a blender until it is smooth.

This sauce goes particularly well with roast rack of lamb.

## White Sauce with Chives

SERVES 4–6

| |
|---|
| 400 ml/14 fl oz white fish stock (see recipe p 41) |
| 175 ml/6 fl oz Noilly Prat |
| 150 ml/¼ pt good white Burgundy |
| 225 g/8 oz shallots, finely chopped |
| 75 g/3 oz butter |
| 225 g/8 oz white part of leeks, chopped |
| 250 ml/8 fl oz water |
| 1 litre/1¾ pt double cream |
| 85 ml/3 fl oz Sauternes |
| 2 heaped tbsp chives |
| extra chives for sprinkling |

**1.** Put the fish stock, Noilly Prat, white Burgundy and shallots in a copper saucepan and reduce over a moderate heat to 1 tbsp of liquid.

**2.** Place the butter, chopped leeks and water in a separate pan, and cook until reduced to 3 or 4 tbsp of liquid. Pass through a fine sieve and retain this concentrated liquid.

**3.** Add the liquid from the leeks to the shallots in the copper saucepan, along with the cream, Sauternes and chives.

**4.** Bring the mixture to the boil, watching carefully to ensure that the cream heats through without reducing.

**5.** Just before serving, add some freshly chopped chives to give a green speckled effect.

This sauce goes well with fish like turbot, sole, scallops or brill that have been very simply steamed. It would combine well with a carefully warmed tomato coulis (see recipe page 36).

# Richard Shepherd
## on
## Soups & Sauces

Richard Shepherd seems always to have a glass of champagne and a Gauloise in a holder in his hands and invariably a smile on his face. As director and head chef at Langan's Brasserie, he has good reason to be content. Langan's is in the heart of London's West End. The dining area is a vast, elegant, Art Deco room crammed with pictures, palms, mirrors and overhead fans. Actor Michael Caine, who has shares in the restaurant, often brings his friends and – together with the original owner, Peter Langan, famous for his impudence and his capacity for champagne – makes Langan's a honey-pot for the busy gossip columnists of Fleet Street. The atmosphere is bustly and very French, the food is good and the menu enormous, revolving around 200 dishes. 'Some of our customers come here three or four times a week, so I have to give them a choice,' Richard Shepherd explains.

He has carefully monitored customer tastes during his five years at Langan's and produced one of those rare menus where everything is tempting. Richard started with just seven first courses, seven main dishes and seven desserts, and slowly built up a repertoire as he pulled the restaurant back together. For when he arrived at Langan's from a very successful run as head chef at the Capital Hotel, London, Langan's was 'a shambles, a pretty near disaster'. The morale of the staff – those who had bothered to stay – was at its lowest ebb and there was no money to pay them. The food was atrocious and the business heavily in debt. Gradually Richard sorted through the debris (with the help of his younger brother Michael, an ex-VAT-inspector) and built up a new system in the kitchen. The challenge was the attraction. At the Capital, Richard had enjoyed the luxury of cooking to order. At Langan's he caters for 500 or 600 people a day.

From a tiny office, Richard can survey his kitchen. In front of him are the meat and fish sections and the massive gas-fired ovens; to the left the vegetable and pastry sections; and to the right the swing doors to the dining area. There is a feeling of gathering tension every morning at Langan's. Stocks are simmering at eight o'clock (barely five hours after the evening shift has gone home) and soon afterwards Richard begins his sauces. Sixty egg yolks make up the five or six gallons of hollandaise used every day. From this basic mixture comes béarnaise and Langan's famous anchovy sauce to accompany the hot spinach soufflé. Then there is duck gravy, lyonnaise, veal gravy, brown sauce – the list is endless. Preparing sauces in advance is one of the compromises Richard has had to make. There is no time to make them to order.

Richard realizes that he is only the co-ordinator and that a successful day depends on the co-operation of everyone. But, like so many cooks, he is a perfectionist, and tempers fray when he sees someone prepare his food less than perfectly. There is a postcard on the kitchen wall: 'The management regret staff found dead from exhaustion will be sacked on the spot.'

He has a vested interest in high standards. He admits his heart is in his mouth as he mounts the stairs after a service to say hello to his regular customers, and this is when he realizes that he is more than a cook. 'To cater for people eating out, cooks should really start out front at the tables with the customers and work back towards the kitchen.'

Richard spent four years at the Savoy Hotel, under the stern eye of Silvino Trompeto, 'a tough disciplinarian who demanded respect, always looked immaculate, but who never did any cooking'. From him, Richard learned the business side of cooking – the ordering of food, the organization of people and the general administration of a large kitchen. In contrast, Pierre Pernet, the head chef at La Réserve de Beaulieu, captivated him with his flair and, especially, his versatility. 'Put him on any section – meat, fish – and he'd excel himself.' Taking the ingredients of Trompeto's business acumen and the all-round skills of Pernet is perhaps the recipe for Richard's own success.

To try to improve the second-class image of cooks in Britain, Anton Mosimann, head chef of the Dorchester, started a group in 1976 called Club Nine. Richard became a member. It is an exclusive but informal group of chefs which meets once a month to talk about food and the problems of the industry. Richard often finds himself giving work opportunities to students from the college of another member, John Huber, and other restaurants connected with the club. It is only by moving around that apprentice chefs can gain the experience they need.

Apart from his own teachers, Richard has no cooking heroes. He found a meal at the famous Paul Bocuse's restaurant very disappointing. But then he is very suspicious of restaurants in France that take credit cards. He tries to avoid them and is certain he has eaten better meals as a result. Trends in cooking leave him unmoved. 'It's all been done before in one form or another, so when people start talking about *cuisine minceur* or *nouvelle*, I'm sorry but I find it a bit of a joke.' It may sound an odd criticism to make about cooks but Richard finds one of the industry's biggest problems is that cooks often don't know enough about food. 'They don't go out to eat – and when they do it's junk food – and so they don't know what food should taste like.' This accounts for French cooks having a head start over British. Eating out in France is almost a weekend institution, and children become accustomed from a very early age to the taste of a good béarnaise or hollandaise sauce. It amazes Richard to watch young English cooks working: 'I've seen them make a soup from beginning to end without ever tasting it.' But even if they do they won't know what to compare the taste with. Unlike the French (Richard has a ready comparison in his Gallic in-laws), British families don't talk about food, about new dishes and new tastes: 'It's as if they'll sound greedy if they do.'

Beneath Richard's often flippant exterior is a dedicated worker trying to produce haute cuisine on a massive scale. This may sound impossible, but the crowded and cheerful atmosphere in Langan's every night is proof enough that Richard Shepherd's style of cooking is the next best thing.

## Brown or White Stock

| |
|---|
| 1 kg/2 lb 3 oz beef, veal or chicken bones |
| 225 g/8 oz mixed vegetables (carrots, celery, onions, leeks), chopped |
| bouquet garni (bay leaf, thyme, parsley stalks, peppercorns) |
| 2.3 litres/4 pt water |

The basic difference betwen white and brown stock is that for white stock the bones and vegetables are left raw, and for brown stock they are coloured, either by roasting or by frying. Stocks must not boil too fast or too slowly, but should be kept simmering and well skimmed. Tomatoes and mushroom trimmings may be added to brown stock to improve the flavour.

**1.** Place the bones, vegetables and herbs in a stock pot – the bones should be put on top of the vegetables so that they keep well down. Cover with cold water and bring to the boil quickly. (Use cold water so that any fat and impurities rise to the surface and can be skimmed off.)
**2.** Reduce the heat so that the stock simmers, and cook for 3–4 hours, skimming frequently.
**3.** Strain when cooked – if the bones and vegetables are left in the stock it may turn sour.

## Fish Stock

| |
|---|
| 1 kg/2 lb 3 oz fish bones (sole or turbot preferably, but do not mix oily fish with white fish) |
| 100 g/4 oz onion, thinly sliced |
| 25 g/1 oz butter |
| bouquet garni (see previous recipe) |
| juice of ½ lemon |
| 2.3 litres/4 pt water |

**1.** Melt the butter in a large saucepan. Add the onions, well-washed fish bones and all the remaining ingredients. Cover with greaseproof paper and the lid of the pan and sweat the vegetables for a few minutes without letting them colour.
**2.** Remove the lid and paper, add cold water and bring to the boil quickly. Skim, reduce the heat and simmer for about 20 minutes.
**3.** Strain and use when required.

## Cream of Cauliflower Soup

| SERVES 4 |
|---|
| 225 g/8 oz raw cauliflower |
| a *mirepoix* of 100 g/4 oz each of onions, leeks and celery, chopped into small dice |
| 50 g/2 oz potato, peeled and chopped |
| 50 g/2 oz butter |
| 50 g/2 oz flour |
| bouquet garni (bay leaf, thyme, parsley stalks, peppercorns) |
| 600 ml/1 pt white stock |
| 600 ml/1 pt milk |
| double cream to taste |

**1.** In a large saucepan, sweat the cauliflower, *mirepoix* and potato in the butter until they are transparent but not coloured.
**2.** Stir in the flour and cook gently for 5 minutes.
**3.** Add the bouquet garni, stock and milk, and simmer for about 30 minutes. Strain the liquid.
**4.** Pass the mixture through a *mouli* or food processor until it is thick and creamy.
**5.** Add this to the strained liquid, stir well and check the seasoning. Serve with a little cream.

# La Soupe aux Moules

*Mussel Soup*

SERVES 4

| |
|---|
| 3 litres/5¼ pt mussels |
| 2 onions, finely chopped |
| 1 bay leaf |
| dash of white wine |
| 3 cloves of garlic, crushed |
| 2 tbsp olive oil |
| 2 tomatoes, skinned, de-seeded and chopped |
| white part of 1 leek, thinly sliced |
| 600 ml/1 pt fish stock |
| pinch of saffron |
| pepper |
| 1 tbsp rice |
| salt |
| a little chopped parsley |

**1.** Clean the mussels and wash them well.
**2.** Place them in a wide-bottomed pan with 1 finely chopped onion, the bay leaf, the white wine and 1 crushed clove of garlic. Cover with a lid and cook over a high heat, shaking the pan from time to time until the mussels have all opened. (Discard any that refuse to open.)
**3.** Remove the mussels from their shells, de-beard them and place on one side.
**4.** Strain the liquid through a fine sieve and also keep to one side.
**5.** Pour the oil into a clean pan, add the other finely chopped onion, and sweat for 2 minutes, without letting the onion colour.
**6.** Add the tomatoes, remaining garlic and leek and sweat for a further 2 minutes.
**7.** Add the liquid from the mussels and the fish stock, saffron and pepper. (Do not add any salt yet, as it may not be needed.) Bring to the boil, skim and sprinkle in the rice.
**8.** When the rice is cooked, add the mussels, check seasoning and sprinkle with parsley.

# Crab Bisque

SERVES 4

| |
|---|
| 450–700 g/1–1½ lb crab (with fingers removed and shell and claws broken down into smaller pieces) |
| a *mirepoix* of 100 g/4 oz each of onions, leeks, celery and carrots, chopped into small dice |
| 50 g/2 oz butter |
| bouquet garni (bay leaf, thyme, parsley stalks, peppercorns) |
| 50 g/2 oz tomato purée |
| 600 ml/1 pt white stock |
| 600 ml/1 pt fish stock |
| 50 g/2 oz rice |
| 4 tbsp Cognac |
| 4 tbsp white wine |
| double cream to taste |

**1.** Sweat the vegetables in the butter with the crab pieces until the vegetables are tender.
**2.** Add the bouquet garni, tomato purée, Cognac, wine and stock. Then add the rice and simmer for 45 minutes.
**3.** Strain off the liquid and discard the large, tough pieces of crab shell, but pulverize the remainder into a paste. Pass the crab paste through a sieve to remove any sharp pieces of shell, then add to the liquid.
**4.** Return the soup to the heat and bring to the boil again.
**5.** Check the seasoning and consistency, which should be fairly thick. If it is too thin, add *beurre manié*: mash a little flour and butter (a dessert-spoon of each) together and add a little at a time to the liquid in small knobs, stirring until the desired consistency is reached and the butter is well amalgamated.
**6.** Serve the soup with a dash of cream.

# La Soupe à l'Oignon

## Onion Soup

SERVES 4

| | |
|---|---|
| 5 onions | |
| 65 g/2½ oz butter | |
| 25 g/1 oz oil | |
| salt | |
| pepper | |
| 20 g/¾ oz flour | |
| 900 ml/1½ pt chicken or veal stock | |
| 1 French loaf | |
| 1 clove of garlic | |
| a little grated nutmeg | |
| 40 g/1½ oz Gruyère cheese, grated | |

**1.** Peel and thinly slice the onions.
**2.** Heat the butter and oil together, add the onions and cook until tender and slightly coloured. Season with salt and pepper.
**3.** Add the flour and mix in well, making sure the roux does not burn.
**4.** Carefully add the stock, a little at a time so that it does not form lumps. When all the stock has been added, allow to simmer for 30 minutes, skimming from time to time.
**5.** Slice the French bread, rub it with the clove of garlic, chop into croutons and toast.
**6.** When the soup is ready, check the seasoning and add a little grated nutmeg.
**7.** Float the croutons on top, cover with the grated cheese and grill, so that the Gruyère forms a golden crust. Serve.

A little white wine or port may be added to the soup to enrich the flavour.

# Hollandaise Sauce

SERVES 4–6

| | |
|---|---|
| 175 g/6 oz butter, clarified (see below) | |
| 2 tbsp water | |
| 3 egg yolks | |
| juice of ½ lemon | |
| salt | |
| cayenne pepper | |

**1.** To clarify the butter, melt it in a saucepan and skim off the froth. Pour the remaining butter into a dish and leave the milky residue behind. Cool until tepid.
**2.** Meanwhile, whisk the water and the egg yolks in a *bain-marie* or double saucepan until the mixture is creamy and the whisk leaves a trail on the bottom of the pan. This may take 5 or more minutes. Keep checking the temperature – if it is too hot take the pan out of the water bath and continue whisking until cooler.
**3.** Take the pan off the heat and whisk in the tepid butter, a few drops at a time (if you add too much too quickly the mixture will curdle).
**4.** Finally, add a little lemon juice. Taste for seasoning and add salt and cayenne pepper.

If curdling does occur, this means that the temperature is too hot or too cold. Take a clean aluminium bowl and add 1 tbsp cold water. Gradually whisk the curdled mixture into the water. If this fails to improve the sauce, take a clean pan and whisk 1 new egg yolk with a little water until creamy, then gradually whisk in the curdled mixture.

If the mixture is too thick, this means the temperature is too high – add a few drops of cold water.

If the mixture does not thicken, increase the heat a little or cook the sauce for slightly longer.

## Sauce Maltaise

Add the blanched, shredded peel and juice of 1 orange to 300 ml/½ pt of the basic hollandaise mixture (see previous recipe).

This sauce goes well with any grilled white fish.

## Sauce Anchois

### Anchovy Sauce

Make a purée of 3 or 4 anchovy fillets, warm them in 2 tbsp water, and add to 300 ml/½ pt of the basic hollandaise mixture (see recipe page 43).

This sauce is used as an accompaniment to Richard Shepherd's famous spinach soufflé, and can be used with other flavoured soufflés or grilled fish dishes.

## Sauce Moutarde

### Mustard Sauce

Mix together ½ tsp each of English and Dijon mustard and add this to 300 ml/½ pt of the basic hollandaise mixture (see recipe page 43).

This is a good sauce for any white fish.

## Béarnaise Sauce

| 300 ml/½ pt hollandaise sauce (see recipe p 43) |
| --- |
| 3 tbsp wine vinegar |
| 3 tbsp white wine |
| 3 shallots, finely chopped |
| 1 tbsp tarragon, finely chopped (optional) |
| 10 crushed peppercorns |

1. Bring all the ingredients except the hollandaise sauce to the boil and reduce mixture until just about 2 tbsp are left. Strain and cool.
2. Discard the shallot mixture. Add the strained juices to the basic hollandaise sauce and, if desired, add the finely chopped tarragon.

This is a delicious sauce with grilled steak, lamb, chicken or fish.

## Sauce Choron

Follow the recipe for the béarnaise sauce (above) but use 1 tbsp concentrated tomato purée instead of the tarragon.

This sauce is suitable for grilled meat or fish.

## Sauce Paloise

Follow the same recipe as for béarnaise sauce (above) but use 1 tbsp mint in place of the tarragon.

This sauce is good with grills, particularly lamb, duck or fish.

## Sauce Bordelaise

SERVES 4–6

| |
|---|
| **50 g/2 oz shallots, chopped** |
| **pinch of crushed peppercorns** |
| **1 sprig of thyme** |
| **1 bay leaf** |
| **150 ml/¼ pt red wine** |
| **900 ml–1 litre/1½–1¾ pt brown stock (see recipe p 41)** |
| **½ tsp fecule (potato starch)** |
| **50 g/2 oz butter** |

**1.** Place the shallots, peppercorns, herbs and wine in a saucepan. Bring to the boil and reduce by three-quarters.
**2.** Reduce the brown stock to 300 ml/½ pt and thicken slightly with the arrowroot to form a *jus-lié*.
**3.** Add the *jus-lié* to the wine mixture and simmer for 20–30 minutes.
**4.** Correct the seasoning to taste, then pass the liquid through a fine sieve.
**5.** Reheat, add the butter in knobs, mix well and serve.

This sauce goes well with fish or red meat.

## Sauce Chasseur

SERVES 4–6

| |
|---|
| **50 g/2 oz butter** |
| **50 g/2 oz shallots, chopped** |
| **100 g/4 oz button mushrooms, sliced** |
| **200 ml/7 fl oz dry white wine** |
| **175 g/6 oz tomatoes skinned, de-seeded and chopped** |
| **300 ml/½ pt *jus-lié* made from brown stock thickened with fecule (see previous recipe)** |
| **1 tbsp tarragon, chopped** |
| **1 tbsp parsley, chopped** |

**1.** Melt the butter in a saucepan and sweat the shallots until soft.
**2.** Add the sliced mushrooms, cover and cook for 2–3 minutes.
**3.** Add the wine, bring the liquid to the boil and reduce by half.
**4.** Add the tomatoes, then stir in the *jus-lié* and simmer the mixture for 15 minutes.
**5.** Add the tarragon and parsley, check the seasoning, and serve.

This sauce goes well with chicken or red meat.

## Fillets of Sole with White Wine Sauce

SERVES 4

| |
|---|
| **2 sole, 450–550 g/1–1¼ lb each** |
| **25 g/1 oz chopped shallot** |
| **salt** |
| **pepper** |
| **150 ml/¼ pt fish stock (see recipe p 41)** |
| **150 ml/¼ pt dry white wine** |
| **juice of ¼ lemon** |
| **150 ml/¼ pt double cream** |
| **75 g/3 oz butter** |

**1.** Fillet and trim the sole.
**2.** Place in a buttered earthenware dish, on top of a bed of chopped shallot, and season. Add the fish stock, white wine and lemon juice. Cover with buttered paper and poach in a 190°C/375°F/Gas Mark 5 oven for 5–10 minutes.
**3.** Drain the liquid into a saucepan and place the fillets on a serving dish. Add half the cream to the liquid and boil until reduced by half.
**4.** Take the pan off the heat and whisk in the butter in small knobs. Add the rest of the cream and check seasoning. Coat the fillets with the sauce and serve at once.

# *Joyce Molyneux*
## *— on Fish —*

'We went to congratulate the chef and found her cleaning the oven,' revealed the *Good Food Guide* in their 1985 issue. After spending a week in her kitchen at the Carved Angel restaurant in Dartmouth, it is clear that Joyce is one of life's workers. Joyce is unmarried, 54 and has been cooking for 35 years. 'I wouldn't like to count the number of chickens I have cooked.' She reminds me of Ingrid Bergman in the film where she led hundreds of children over the mountains to safety – she has a scrubbed, open, honest face and, like so many cooks I have met, is imbued with a very generous spirit.

Her joy in cooking came from her father, who was a scientist, and it was with his support that she weathered the attempts to put her off a career in cooking. In 1947 it was rare indeed for women to cook for a living unless it was in the local school or factory canteen, but Joyce in that year began a domestic science course in Birmingham. It was run by a Scottish 'mafia' and the syllabus was devised for middle-class ladies who employed someone to do the 'rougher things in the kitchen', leaving them free to make scones of every variety. Joyce left in 1949 and after a miserable year in industry moved to a restaurant in Stratford-upon-Avon and then in 1959 to the Hole-in-the-Wall in Bath.

Until she worked there with George Perry Smith, Joyce had never been expected to have opinions at all. But rare though women were in other restaurant kitchens, at the 'Hole' they outnumbered men, and in the early 1970s Joyce was made a partner. Mr Perry Smith, as Joyce called him for the first ten years, was a self-taught disciple of Elizabeth David, whose great work, *French Provincial Cookery*, was published around this time. Many dishes that he had made famous at the Hole-in-the-Wall originated from the books written by this remarkable woman. He says now that his style of cooking, which his own disciples have taken to many small restaurant kitchens across the country, is almost casserole cooking in the sense that he encourages ingredients to blend gently together to produce a final result.

When George moved from Bath to Helford in Cornwall to open the Riverside, a small restaurant with rooms, Joyce went to Dartmouth to run the kitchen at the Carved Angel. The Svengali influence has now relaxed, allowing Joyce to develop her own style of cooking, but the influence of Elizabeth David is certainly evident in all that Joyce cooks – 'somehow she links the home kitchen to the restaurant and she also appreciates good food from any country whatsoever'. Perhaps this last observation explains why some of Joyce's combinations of tastes have been described as 'culinary gymnastics' – like guinea fowl cooked with red wine and pig's trotters; or ox tongue with beetroot and celeriac; or brochettes of beef marinated in ginger and orange and served with spiced aubergines.

On the subject of styles in cooking, Joyce says, 'Perhaps being English is being willing to listen. Unlike the French, who close their ears, we collect styles from all over the world.' Although she admits to being an 'offal foodie' herself, the Carved Angel is renowned for its fish, hardly surprising since every salmon she cooks has actually swum past her front door on its way from the sea to its spawning grounds on Dartmoor. 'Fish according to shopping' on the menu leaves Joyce free to respond to what the sea and river fishermen bring in. Marinaded shark was on the menu when I was in Dartmouth – and I doubt if there are many restaurateurs with the confidence to include *that* as a *plat du jour*. Joyce is particularly proud of the 30 or more food suppliers she has cultivated in the last ten years. A roll-call would take too long here, but there is Patrick Keene, one of only nineteen licence-holders on the River Dart, who brings fresh salmon for the Salmon in Pastry with Ginger and Currants or the Salmon with Samphire and Champagne; or Mr Distin, who runs the local Castle Ferry, who brings Dover sole for a dish of sole with fresh herbs; or Mr Turner who brings rabbits for the rabbit, marinaded in marjoram and lemon, roasted and served with sloe and apple jelly; or Mr Brooks the vet who rears guinea fowl. Her suppliers range from a local woman who will pick wild samphire while walking the dog to professionals like David and Ingrid Lloyd who run a fruit farm in Dittisham. 'People make the mistake of thinking that restaurants need massive amounts of everything.' Half a pound of wild strawberries or puffballs or a handful of wild fennel is welcome, though it requires some ingenuity to put them to good use. Even a sack of rather doubtful peas bought for 50 pence from the local greengrocer made a delicious pea purée for a Best End of Lamb with Onion Sauce. Some people may be irritated by the folksy tag of blackcurrant leaves or rose petals in the recipes but I have to admit that this use of what is growing around us fascinates me. Joyce integrates these unexpected flavours into a sophisticated but refreshing menu which has certainly earned its 'jewel in the West Country' reputation in the *Good Food Guide*.

Following in the George Perry Smith tradition, Joyce employs a predominantly female staff of six whom she describes affectionately as her surrogate children. In line with this family idea, each person is expected to work in all sections of the restaurant – one day waiting at table, the next washing up and cleaning, and a third in the kitchen cooking. By doing each other's jobs, each will respect and understand the pressures on the other. They certainly couldn't have a more patient teacher than Joyce: 'It's lovely seeing them come to work for me and leaving perhaps a year later more confident and better equipped for the job in hand.' The most important lesson they take with them is her respect for good housekeeping and her hatred of waste. They also take with them any recipe they want, for Joyce is delighted to pass on her successes.

She simply likes giving pleasure – that is really why she has been cooking for 35 years. 'And the good thing about cooking is that you get to eat your mistakes. At least they don't live to reproach you for evermore.'

# Scallops with Bacon and White Wine

SERVES 4

| |
|---|
| 8 scallops |
| pepper |
| flour for dusting |
| 50 g/2 oz butter |
| 2 shallots |
| 2 rashers of streaky green bacon, cut in small pieces |
| 150 ml/¼ pt fish stock |
| 150 ml/¼ pt white wine |
| 2 tbsp chopped parsley |
| salt |

1. Slice the scallops thinly into two or three pieces and season them with pepper only. Dust lightly with flour.
2. Melt the butter in a pan, add the shallots and fry a little before adding the bacon. Cook for a further 3 minutes.
3. Add the scallops and cook gently for about 1 minute on each side.
4. Add the fish stock, white wine and chopped parsley. Cook for another minute.
5. Check seasoning and serve with a slice of toasted brioche (see recipe page 119).

# Gravadbass

Sea bass prepared in a similar manner to *gravadlax*.

SERVES 4

| |
|---|
| 2.3 kg/5 lb sea bass |
| handful of finely chopped dill |
| marinade of 2 tbsp sea salt, 2 tbsp sugar and 1 tbsp crushed peppercorns |

1. Fillet the bass.
2. Sprinkle one-third of the marinade mixture and a little of the dill on to a china dish.
3. Lay a fillet on the plate, skin side downwards. Sprinkle with another third of the mixture and more dill.
4. Lay the other fillet on top, and add the rest of the mixture and dill.
5. Cover the dish with cling film, then a piece of cardboard and weights of about 2 kg/5 lb. Leave for 24 hours.
6. Slice as for smoked salmon and serve with a mustardy mayonnaise.

# Lobster Mallorquina

SERVES 4

| |
|---|
| 2 × 675-g/1½-lb lobsters, cooked |
| 15 g/½ oz butter |
| 15 g/½ oz flour |
| 150 ml/¼ pt single cream |
| 25 ml/1 fl oz dry sherry |
| salt |
| pepper |
| squeeze of lemon juice |
| dash of brandy |
| 2 large eggs, separated |
| butter for sautéing |

1. Make a roux with the butter and flour, then add the single cream to make a sauce.
2. Remove from the heat and season with the sherry, salt, pepper and lemon juice. Add brandy to taste. (It should taste quite strong as it will be softened later by the addition of eggs.)
3. Add the egg yolks, mixing them in well.
4. Split the lobsters and remove the flesh from the claws and tail, cutting it into scallops.
5. Put the empty half-shells of lobster on to a baking tray.

**6.** Sprinkle the lobster flesh with a little sherry and salt and pepper, and warm gently in a little butter.

**7.** Whip the egg whites stiffly and fold into the sauce.

**8.** Put a little of the soufflé sauce into the bottom of each shell, divide the lobster between the four shells, and coat carefully with the balance of the sauce.

**9.** Sprinkle with a few lobster eggs (if available) and bake in a hot oven (230°C/450°F/Gas Mark 8) for 5–8 minutes until golden-brown. Serve immediately.

# Red Mullet with Anchovies and Orange

| SERVES 4 |
| --- |
| 4 red mullet, about 225 g/8 oz each |
| 12 anchovy fillets |
| seasoned flour |
| 120 ml/4 fl oz orange juice |
| 60 ml/4 tbsp diced fresh tomato |
| chopped parsley |
| 1 orange, sectioned |

**1.** Cut 4 anchovy fillets into quarters.

**2.** Make 2 slashes on each side of the mullet and put a piece of anchovy in each.

**3.** Dip the fish in seasoned flour and grill it under a very hot grill for 5 minutes each side. Place on a serving dish.

**4.** Put the orange juice, tomato and rest of the anchovy fillets in a grill pan and reduce to make a sauce. Taste.

**5.** Pour the sauce round the mullet and decorate with parsley and orange sections.

# Mussels Stuffed with Spinach

| SERVES 4 |
| --- |
| 600-ml/1-pt measure mussels per person |
| 50 ml/2 fl oz white wine |
| 225 g/8 oz spinach |
| 25 g/1 oz thick béchamel sauce |
| salt |
| pepper |
| nutmeg |
| 50 g/2 oz soft breadcrumbs |
| 50 g/2 oz butter |

**1.** Put the cleaned mussels into a pan with a little white wine, cover and cook until they open. Remove the top shell of each mussel.

**2.** Purée the lightly cooked spinach with the thick béchamel. Season with salt, pepper and nutmeg.

**3.** Top the mussels with this mixture, using a palette knife to give an even finish.

**4.** Sprinkle with the soft breadcrumbs and a dribble of melted butter.

**5.** Bake in a hot oven (210°C/425°F/Gas Mark 7) for 5 minutes and then finish under the grill.

**Nico Ladenis** *Fish Soup (page 35)*

**Richard Shepherd** *Cream of Cauliflower Soup (page 41)*

## John Dory with Orange and Mushroom Stuffing

SERVES 4

| |
|---|
| 4 John Dory, about 450 g/1 lb each with heads removed |
| 2 oranges |
| 50 g/2 oz shallots, finely chopped |
| 50 g/2 oz butter |
| 225 g/8 oz mushrooms, sliced |
| 50 ml/2 fl oz white wine |
| salt |
| pepper |
| 225 ml/8 fl oz double cream |
| chopped parsley, to garnish |

**1.** Peel 1 orange with a potato peeler. Blanch the strips of peel and shred finely.

**2.** Section both oranges.

**3.** Sweat the shallots in the butter until soft, add the mushrooms and cook until fairly dry.

**4.** Add the shredded orange peel and half the orange sections. Season to taste.

**5.** Stuff the Dory with this mixture, pressing in well.

**6.** Put the fish in a baking dish with the white wine round it. Season, cover with lid or foil and bake in a cool oven (150°C/300°F/Gas Mark 2) for 20–30 minutes until cooked.

**7.** Remove the fish to a serving dish. Take off the top skin.

**8.** Reduce the juices by one-third over a fast heat and finish with the double cream. Taste, adjust seasoning and pour round the fish.

**9.** Decorate with the remaining orange sections and parsley.

## Brill with a Pistachio Mousseline and Vegetables

'An underestimated fish as delicious in its own way as turbot.'

SERVES 4

| |
|---|
| 4 × 175-g/6-oz fillets of brill |
| 150 ml/¼ pt white wine |
| 50 g/2 oz carrots, cut in strips |
| 50 g/2 oz mushrooms, sliced |
| 50 g/2 oz celery, cut in strips |
| 1 oz/25 g butter, to finish |
| few sprigs of chervil, to garnish |

| *For the pistachio mousseline* |
|---|
| 100–125 g/4 oz brill, trimmed from the fillets |
| 15 g/½ oz skinned pistachios |
| 15 g/½ oz chervil |
| 1 egg white |
| salt |
| pepper |
| 150 ml/¼ pt double cream |

**1.** Skin the brill fillets and trim any frill and a little off the tails to give 100 g/4 oz; use this for the mousseline.

**2.** Purée the fish trimmings in a food processor with the pistachios, chervil and egg white.

**3.** Rub through a fine sieve. Season.

**4.** Gradually beat in the cream.

**5.** Sprinkle the vegetables into a buttered oven dish and lay the brill fillets on top. Pipe on the mousseline. Pour in the white wine, cover and cook in a cool oven (140°C/275°F/Gas Mark 1) for about 15 minutes until the fish comes away from the bone when tested.

**6.** Remove the fillets to a serving dish. Reduce the juices by half and add the butter in small knobs to thicken the sauce slightly.

**7.** Pour the sauce round the fish, garnish with chervil and serve.

## Porbeagle Shark with Butter, Lemon and Parsley

SERVES 4

| |
|---|
| 4 × 100-g/4-oz portions of shark cut into escalopes |
| salt |
| pepper |
| 1 lemon |
| 1 tbsp chopped parsley |
| 100 g/4 oz butter |

**1.** Season the fish with salt, pepper and lemon juice.
**2.** Melt the butter in a pan and cook the fish lightly on both sides, sprinkling each side with chopped parsley.
**3.** Serve with a wedge of lemon.

This dish can be finished with black butter (made from butter, white wine vinegar and parsley).

## Salmon in Pastry with Ginger and Currants Served with a Herb and Cream Sauce

SERVES 4

| |
|---|
| 675 g–1 kg/1½–2 lb fresh salmon |
| salt |
| pepper |
| 2–3 pieces of preserved ginger |
| 1 tbsp currants |
| 50 g/2 oz slightly salted butter |
| 225 g/8 oz shortcrust pastry |
| egg for egg wash |

**1.** Fillet the salmon and skin it. Remove any internal bones with a pair of pliers. Divide the fish into two horizontal slices. Season with salt and pepper.
**2.** Rinse the ginger of its syrup. Chop it finely and mix with the currants and butter (which has been allowed to soften). Spread over each slice of fish. Sandwich the fish together.
**3.** Roll out the pastry and wrap it round the salmon to make a neat parcel.
**4.** Egg-wash the pastry and bake for 30–45 minutes depending on size and shape of finished product. Cook for the first 20 minutes at 220°C/425°F/Gas Mark 7 and then reduce to 150°C/300°F/Gas Mark 2 for the remainder of the time. Serve with the herb and cream sauce.

| *Herb and Cream Sauce* |
|---|
| 2 shallots |
| 25 g/1 oz butter |
| 4 tsp chopped parsley |
| 2 tsp chopped chervil |
| 2 tsp tarragon |
| 1 tsp flour |
| 300 ml/½ pt single cream |
| 1 tsp French coarse-grain mustard |
| 1 egg yolk |
| squeeze of lemon juice |
| salt |
| pepper |

**1.** Chop the shallots and sweat them in the butter; add the herbs and cook a little longer.
**2.** Add the flour, mixing well, and then the single cream. Bring gently to the boil, stirring well with a wooden spoon. Cook for about 5 minutes.
**3.** Season, add the mustard, egg yolk and lemon juice, and recheck seasoning.

**Joyce Molyneux** *Top, Scallops with Bacon and White Wine (page 48); left, Mussels Stuffed with Spinach (page 48); bottom, Lobster Mallorquina (page 48)*

**Joyce Molyneux** *Salmon in Pastry with Ginger and Currants*
*Served with a Herb and Cream Sauce (page 53)*

## Fillets of Dover Sole with Sorrel and Herbs

'This is a very simple, summery dish.'

SERVES 4

| |
|---|
| 4 × 150-g/5-oz Dover sole fillets |
| salt |
| pepper |
| lemon juice |
| a little flour |
| 50 g/2 oz butter |
| handful of chopped herbs including plenty of sorrel, parsley, chives, chervil and fennel |

**1.** Season the sole with salt, pepper and lemon juice, and flour lightly.
**2.** Melt the butter in a pan, add the sole and fry gently on one side for 1–2 minutes.
**3.** Add the chopped herbs before turning over and frying on the other side until firm but not dry.

## Salt Cod with Almonds and Pine Kernels

'Salt cod, I know, is mostly used in France and Spain, but I feel sure holidaymakers have good memories of it – and even bring some back home. I know I always do!'

SERVES 4

| |
|---|
| 450 g/1 lb salt cod, soaked for 48 hours – changing the water twice |
| 150 ml/¼ pt olive oil |
| 50 g/2 oz roasted almonds |
| 50 g/2 oz pine kernels |
| 3 cloves of garlic |
| 350 g/12 oz tomatoes, skinned |
| 150 ml/¼ pt white wine |
| 150 ml/¼ pt fish stock |
| parsley, to garnish |

**1.** Drain the salt cod and dry it on kitchen paper.
**2.** Flour and fry it in the olive oil to brown both sides.
**3.** Purée the almonds, pine kernels, garlic and tomatoes in a blender. Add the mixture to the cod, with the white wine and fish stock. Cook gently until the cod is tender.
**4.** Check seasoning. Finish with a little chopped parsley.

Serve with a slice of fried bread which has been rubbed with garlic.

## Salmon with Red Wine and Mushrooms

'Salmon, being a rich, meaty fish, stands up to the red wine very well, making a very balanced combination.'

SERVES 4

| |
|---|
| 4 × 175-g/6-oz salmon steaks |
| 225 g/8 oz button mushrooms |
| salt |
| pepper |
| 250 ml/8 fl oz red Burgundy |
| 50–75 g/2–3 oz butter, to finish sauce |
| chopped parsley, to garnish |

**1.** Put the salmon steaks into a buttered dish with the mushrooms, quartered, and a little salt and pepper. Pour the red wine over them. Cover and cook gently on top or in a cool oven (140°C/275°F/Gas Mark 1) for 10–15 minutes until just cooked.
**2.** Place the salmon on a serving dish, reduce the juices in the pan by half, and finish with a few knobs of butter and some chopped parsley. Pour over the salmon and serve.

# *Anton Mosimann*
## *on Fish*

Anton Mosimann knew when he was six that he wanted to be a cook, and that single-minded devotion to his craft explains the man and his success. He was born in Solothurn near Bern, Switzerland, in 1947, where his parents combined a restaurant and a farm business. When he was five they moved from the farm to a restaurant twenty miles away. On the days it closed, the child would cook for the staff. At eight years old he remembers turning out quite a respectable spaghetti or cheese fondue.

From the beginning Anton knew that he wanted to be head chef of a large hotel and exactly what he would have to do to achieve his goal. His first job was at the Hotel Baeren, a 30-bedroom establishment in Twan. Tucked beside a beautiful lake, the restaurant was famous for its freshwater fish. Perch Meunière and féra (a cross between a trout and a perch) poached in white wine were local specialities. Anton can remember the delicious smell of wild mushroom sauce from Côtes de Veau aux Morilles. Some people have visual memories, but Anton's are aromatic. After the Hotel Baeren every job seemed easy. His first experience of haute cusine came with his next move, to the Palace Hotel at Villars in 1964. Here Anton learned that, in matters of elegant cooking, precision is all-important.

With that same exactness Anton planned every job that followed. He chose what he wanted to learn, the chefs from whom he wanted to learn, and made sure that he did it. Anton often tells his chefs at the Dorchester that a 'good cook is an eternal apprentice', and that is true in his own case. After working in the Canadian Pavilion during Expo 1967, the offers of work began. But Anton did not yet consider himself ready. Even his marriage had to wait until he had reached his goal – the highest Swiss award: Chef de Cuisine Diplome. He won that in 1973, the youngest chef to do so – and got married the same year. But his pastrywork still did not come up to his own standards so he took a winter job as a commis pâtissier in Gstaad to master the finer points of the art. When Anton came to the Dorchester in 1975 he spent a year under Eugene Kauffler, head chef there for the previous 25 years. A year later it was Anton's turn. He became head chef at the age of 29 – the youngest man ever to be appointed.

There are more than 80 staff in the Dorchester kitchens, banquets for hundreds to arrange

**Joyce Molyneux** *Top, Brill with a Pistachio Mousseline and Vegetables (page 52); bottom, John Dory with Orange and Mushroom Stuffing (page 52)*

**Anton Mosimann** *Salade de Homard avec Champignons Sauvages (page 64)*

every day, not to mention the idiosyncrasies of the hotel's clients that have to be accommodated. Despite the fact that it is such an enormous operation, it is one that Anton manages with skill: he prides himself on knowing each of his staff by name. 'If I go round in the morning and I see an unhappy face I like to know why, because it could be very dangerous for me; he could put too much salt in the soup.'

Anton tries to cook for at least a couple of hours each day: 'It's not fair if people are sweating behind a stove while I'm in my office, nice and cool. I like to sweat with them.' He has devised a way of ensuring standards don't slip while he's away, at least as far as presentation is concerned. Reference photographs of individual dishes help the cooks ensure there is a very definite look to each Dorchester plate. Anton's food is certainly the prettiest to be seen – and perhaps reflects the time he spent cooking in Japan. There is a deliberate yet delicate quality about it, a balance of colour and texture.

When he cooks, Anton clearly follows the dictum of Auguste Escoffier: *'La bonne cuisine est celle où les choses ont le goût de ce qu'elles sont'* – good food is food that tastes of what it is. The thick sauces of the classic dishes have been made lighter (they should be eaten like soup, with a spoon, claims Anton), the vegetables now merely flirt with boiling water and the portions are altogether smaller. Anton calls this way of cooking *cuisine moderne* – nothing really new but a continuing refinement of ingredients. Perhaps more than any of the other twelve cooks, Anton is a devotee of nouvelle cuisine. But while he believes in lighter, simpler, smaller, dishes, he also believes in four, five or six courses. 'It's much more joy. I think eating should be combined with fun.' And in aid of fun, Anton created a Menu Surprise for the Dorchester Grillroom – a six-course meal for a set price per head. Dishes are based on what ingredients are

of good value in the market that day, so there is a delicious sense of mystery and anticipation as each course arrives.

But happy though he is to take up the challenge of refining cooking processes, Anton is aware too that British cooks must help each other – to foster good standards, new ideas and above all improve their mediocre image. To this end, in 1976 he conceived the idea of Club Nine – a group of nine chefs, of whom eight still meet at least once a month to exchange ideas, suppliers, even staff, in the cause of good cooking.

For Anton, cooking is a serious business – demanding what he calls a 'holy devotion'. The cook should concentrate exclusively on what he is doing. 'If you can't, it's better you don't even start' is Anton's advice. His words echo those of that famous cook, Fernand Point. Known as the father of nouvelle cuisine, he instructed great cooks like Bocuse, Outhier, Bise, Chapel and the Troisgros brothers: 'As far as cuisine is concerned one must read everything – in order to retain in the end just a little bit.' Anton has collected more than 4000 cookery books in this quest to learn 'just a little bit'. The most coveted is a first edition of Escoffier's *Pâtissière Parisienne*. 'Escoffier has done so much for cooks. He gave us recipes, he gave us status.'

To be head chef of a grand and famous hotel was Anton's aim when he started as a boy of fifteen. What happens next? Anton receives about half a dozen attractive offers a year – perhaps one that he might consider seriously. 'I need action and I love to organize,' he says, so it is hard to imagine Anton settling for a small family restaurant. He is concerned too to share his knowledge – and his books – with other cooks and he would like to create a museum of cuisine.

One thing is certain about Anton's future: he'll never be idle and he'll always be of service wherever he is.

## Rendez-Vous de Fruits de Mer

*Seafood in a Chive Sauce*

SERVES 4

| |
|---|
| **4 large scallops in shells** |
| **8 scampi removed from shells** |
| **150 g/5 oz salmon, cut into pieces of 15 g/½ oz each** |
| **150 g/5 oz turbot, cut into pieces of 15 g/½ oz each** |
| **salt** |
| **pepper** |
| **cayenne pepper** |
| **20 g/¾ oz each of carrot, leek and celery, cut into julienne strips** |
| **85 g/3¼ oz butter** |
| **200 ml/7 fl oz fish stock** |
| **200 ml/7 fl oz dry white wine** |
| **450 ml/¾ pt double cream** |
| **2 tbsp Noilly Prat** |
| **12–15 chives, finely chopped** |

**1.** Open the scallops. (Putting them on a hot plate for a few minutes will help open them completely.) Remove the scallops and red roes with a soupspoon, separate them, and wash carefully. Cut the scallops in half and place on a cloth to dry.
**2.** Season the scampi, salmon and turbot pieces.
**3.** Sweat the carrot, leek and celery in 20 g/¾ oz butter for a minute or two. Add the turbot and scampi and continue to sweat, then add the salmon and scallops and sweat for another 1–2 minutes.
**4.** Add the fish stock and white wine, bring to the boil and simmer for 2 minutes.
**5.** Remove the seafood and vegetables and keep them warm.
**6.** Reduce the stock by half, add the cream and Noilly Prat, and reduce a little more.

**7.** Return the seafood and vegetables to the sauce, and sprinkle with chives.
**8.** Finish the sauce with the remaining butter to give a fine sheen: drop the butter in small knobs into the sauce and stir gently until melted and incorporated. Season with salt and pepper. Serve in individual ramekins.

## Coquille St Jacques au Safran

*Scallops with Saffron Sauce*

SERVES 4

| |
|---|
| **16 large scallops** |
| **10 g/¼ oz chopped shallot** |
| **20 g/¾ oz butter** |
| **salt** |
| **pepper** |
| **150 ml/¼ pt fish stock** |
| **150 ml/¼ pt white wine** |
| **300 ml/½ pt double cream** |
| **a few saffron threads** |
| **65 g/2½ oz tomatoes, diced** |
| **2 tbsp chopped parsley** |

**1.** Remove the scallops from their shells with a soupspoon, separate the white from the red flesh (roes) and wash carefully. Halve the scallops and place on a cloth to dry.
**2.** In a heavy frying pan, sweat the shallot in the butter without letting it brown.
**3.** Add the seasoned scallops and roes, pour in the fish stock and white wine, and simmer for 1 minute. Remove the scallops and keep hot.
**4.** Reduce the stock by half, add the cream and saffron, and reduce to a slightly thickened consistency.
**5.** Add the tomatoes and parsley, and salt and pepper to taste. Return the scallops and roes to the sauce and serve at once.

**Anton Mosimann** *Rendez-Vous de Fruits de Mer (page 61)*

**Anton Mosimann** *Coquille St Jacques au Safran (page 61)*

# Salade de Homard avec Champignons Sauvages

## *Lobster Salad with Wild Mushrooms*

SERVES 4

2 small lobsters (300 g/10 oz each)

1.2 litres/2 pt stock (see below)

200 g/7 oz haricots verts

50 g/2 oz fresh cèpes

50 g/2 oz fresh chanterelles

50 ml/2 fl oz olive oil

8 green asparagus tips

1 small lettuce

2 red chicory heads

4 slices of truffle

16 basil leaves

*For the vinaigrette*

150 ml/¼ pt hazelnut oil

1 tbsp sherry vinegar

10 g/¼ oz finely chopped shallot

salt

freshly ground pepper

*For the stock*

1 litre/1¾ pt water

300 ml/½ pt dry white wine

12 crushed peppercorns

a little thyme

1 bay leaf

50 g/2 oz onion, cut up into small pieces

40 g/1½ oz carrot, cut up into small pieces

salt

freshly ground pepper

**1.** Prepare the stock first: bring the water and white wine to the boil, add the peppercorns, thyme, bay leaf, onion and carrot, season and simmer for 10 minutes.

**2.** Put the lobsters into the stock and simmer for 5 minutes. Remove and keep lukewarm.

**3.** Wash the haricots verts thoroughly, cook until crisp and then plunge immediately into cold water.

**4.** Wash the cèpes and chanterelles thoroughly and sauté in the olive oil until golden. Keep lukewarm and put to one side.

**5.** Prepare the asparagus tips, and cook until crisp. Keep lukewarm.

**6.** Dry the washed lettuce and arrange attractively on a plate, then the haricots verts, cèpes, chanterelles, chicory and asparagus tips.

**7.** Remove the lobster flesh from the shells, cut into small pieces and arrange on the lettuce and other vegetables.

**8.** Make the seasoned vinaigrette and pour it over the dish. Garnish with slices of truffle and sprinkle with the basil leaves to finish.

It is important that the lobster, cèpes, chanterelles, haricots verts and asparagus tips should still be lukewarm when served.

## Tronçon de Turbot Soufflé aux Écrevisses

### Turbot Steaks with Crayfish

SERVES 4

| |
|---|
| 4 turbot steaks (120 g/4½ oz each) |
| a little finely chopped shallot |
| 150 ml/¼ pt Noilly Prat |
| 300 ml/½ pt fish stock |
| 300 ml/½ pt single cream |
| 40 g/1½ oz butter, to finish |
| 4 chervil sprigs |
| salt |
| pepper |

### For the pike mousseline

| |
|---|
| 250 g/9 oz pike flesh, minced finely |
| cayenne pepper |
| nutmeg |
| 300 ml/½ pt double cream |

### For the garnish

| |
|---|
| 100 g/4 oz cucumber, turned and blanched |
| 4 freshwater crayfish |
| 4 slices of truffle |
| 4 puff pastry fleurons or stars |

**1.** To make the pike mousseline, take the minced pike flesh, season with cayenne and nutmeg, and work in the double cream using a wooden spoon. Press the mixture through a fine sieve and chill on ice or in the fridge.

**2.** Remove the bones but leave the skin on the turbot steaks, then stuff them with the pike mousseline.

**3.** Set the oven to 180°C/350°F/Gas Mark 4. Place the shallot and turbot steaks in a buttered ovenproof dish. Add the Noilly Prat and fish stock. Cover and poach for about 40 minutes or until cooked.

**4.** When cooked, remove the fish and keep it warm.

**5.** Pour the stock into a pan, reduce by half, add the cream and reduce again until it coats the back of a spoon.

**6.** Work the butter into the sauce, a little at a time, to finish it. Add the chervil sprigs and season with salt and pepper.

**7.** Remove the skin from the steaks, arrange on a dish and cover with the sauce. Garnish with blanched cucumber, crayfish which have been warmed in stock, truffle slices and fleurons.

## Queue de Lotte Grillée aux Herbes

### Grilled Monkfish Tail with Fresh Herbs

SERVES 4

| |
|---|
| 4 monkfish tails (200 g/7 oz each), without bones |
| 150 ml/¼ pt olive oil |
| 15 g/½ oz mixed herbs (dill, basil, thyme and marjoram) |
| 1 clove of garlic |
| salt |
| pepper |
| parsley, to garnish |
| 150 ml/¼ pt melted butter |

**1.** Remove the skin from the fish and trim well. Marinate the pieces of fish in the olive oil, mixed herbs, garlic and a little salt and pepper for 1 hour.

**2.** Remove the pieces of fish, season lightly again and brown under the grill for 3–4 minutes each side, basting with the marinade (taking care the herb mixture does not burn).

**3.** Arrange on a hot dish and garnish with the parsley. Serve the melted butter separately.

**Pierre Koffmann** *Top, Lapereau Farci aux Foie Gras, Artichauts et Truffes (page 82); bottom, Le Pigeonneau Rôti au Vinaigre de Framboises et au Chocolat Amer (page 82)*

**Pierre Koffmann** *Poularde Henri IV or Poule au Pot with Chou Farci (page 80)*

## Suprème de Turbot à la Moutarde

*Turbot in a Light Cream Mustard Sauce*

SERVES 4

| |
|---|
| 4 turbot fillets (165 g/5½ oz each) |
| salt |
| freshly ground pepper |
| 1 tsp finely chopped shallot |
| 200 ml/7 fl oz white wine |
| 150 ml/¼ pt fish stock |
| 250 ml/8 fl oz double cream |
| 10 g/¼ oz Dijon mustard |
| 100 g/4 oz butter, to finish |
| a little lemon juice |
| 4 puff pastry fleurons or stars |
| 4 truffle slices |

**1.** Set the oven to 180°C/350°F/Gas Mark 4. Fillet and season the turbot, and place in a buttered shallow dish with the chopped shallots. Add the white wine and fish stock, cover and poach in the oven until soft (4–5 minutes).

**2.** Remove the turbot and keep warm. Pour the stock into a pan and reduce by about half, add 200 ml/7 fl oz cream and reduce further until a slightly thickened consistency is achieved.

**3.** Finish with the mustard and butter, worked in gradually.

**4.** Carefully mix in the remaining cream, whipped thick, and season with salt, pepper and a little lemon juice.

**5.** Arrange the fish on a serving plate, cover with the sauce and brown under the grill. Garnish with the fleurons and slices of truffle.

## Suprème de Sole Philippe

*Fillet of Sole in a White Wine Sauce with Prawns and Mushrooms*

SERVES 4

| |
|---|
| 2 sole (approx 800 g/1¾ lb each) |
| 1 tbsp finely chopped shallot |
| salt |
| freshly ground white pepper |
| 150 ml/¼ pt dry white wine |
| 150 ml/¼ pt fish stock |
| 450 ml/¾ pt double cream |
| 1 tbsp Armagnac |
| 75 g/3 oz butter, to finish sauce |
| 12 red prawns with their heads |
| 50 g/2 oz mushrooms, cut into small strips and lightly poached |
| 4 puff pastry fleurons or stars |

**1.** Set the oven to 180°C/350°F/Gas Mark 4. Remove the skin from both sides of the sole and fillet them.

**2.** Sprinkle a buttered dish with the shallot. Season and fold over the fillets of sole and place them in the dish. Add the white wine and fish stock (reserving 2 tbsp), cover with buttered paper and poach in the oven for about 15 minutes or until tender.

**3.** Remove the sole and keep warm. Pour the stock into a pan and reduce by half.

**4.** Add the cream and continue to reduce until a smooth, slightly thickened consistency is achieved.

**5.** Add the Armagnac, finish gradually with the butter and season with salt and pepper.

**6.** Arrange the fillets of sole on a warmed serving dish and cover with the sauce.

**7.** Warm the prawns in the reserved 2 tbsp stock and use as a garnish, with the poached mushrooms and fleurons.

# Suprème de Haddock Elysée

*Smoked Haddock with Asparagus and Cream Sauce*

SERVES 4

| |
|---|
| 4 haddock fillets (165 g/5½ oz each) |
| 10 g/¼ oz finely chopped shallot |
| 150 ml/¼ pt dry white wine |
| 200 ml/7 fl oz fish stock |
| 450 ml/¾ pt cream |
| 100 g/4 oz tomatoes, diced |
| 75–90 g/3–3½ oz butter |
| salt |
| freshly ground pepper |
| 12 green asparagus tips, blanched |

**1.** Set the oven to 180°C/350°F/Gas Mark 4. Poach the carefully trimmed haddock fillets with the shallot, white wine and fish stock in a buttered dish for about 5 minutes until soft.
**2.** Remove the haddock fillets and keep them warm on a serving dish. Pour the stock into a pan and boil until reduced by about half.
**3.** Add the cream and reduce further to a slightly thickened consistency.
**4.** Add the tomatoes and finish the sauce with 65 g/2½ oz butter, working it in gradually. Season with salt and pepper, and pour over the fillets.
**5.** Warm the asparagus tips in the remaining butter and use as a garnish.

# Filet de Truite Maître Otto Schlegel

*Fillet of Rainbow Trout with a Chive Butter Sauce*

SERVES 4–6

| |
|---|
| 6 rainbow trout (175 g/6 oz each) |
| 10 g/¼ oz celery, cut into slices |
| 10 g/¼ oz leek, cut into small pieces |
| salt |
| freshly ground white pepper |
| 150 ml/¼ pt dry white wine (eg Dezaley) |
| a little cornflour |
| 150 g/5 oz butter, to finish |
| 1 tbsp chives, finely chopped |
| cayenne pepper |

**1.** Set the oven to 180°C/350°F/Gas Mark 4. Gut the fresh trout and fillet them carefully with a sharp knife.
**2.** Place the celery and leek in a buttered dish. Lay the seasoned trout fillets on top, add most of the white wine, cover with buttered paper and poach for about 3 minutes until tender.
**3.** Remove the trout fillets, take off the skin and keep warm. Pour the stock into a pan and reduce by half, then thicken with cornflour.
**4.** Remove the pan from the heat and gradually work in the butter, adding the remaining white wine, to finish the sauce.
**5.** Add the chives to the sauce and season with salt, pepper and cayenne pepper.
**6.** Arrange the trout fillets on a warmed serving dish and cover with the light, delicate sauce. Serve immediately.

**Pierre Koffmann** *Chartreuse d'Agneau au Persil (page 77)*

**Albert and Michel Roux** *Queue de Boeuf aux Echalottes (page 86)*

# Pierre Koffmann
## on Meat

'The smell of cooking is the smell of life' – the words of Pierre Koffmann, chef/patron of La Tante Claire, the restaurant with two Michelin stars near the Embankment in Chelsea. Critics have described him as the 'yardstick by which other chefs in this country are judged', which is heady praise; but I doubt whether Pierre even bothered to read the review, let alone accept the compliment.

Pierre Koffmann is 36, a large, laconic man who seems to have moved almost effortlessly through life to the top of his profession. When he left school in Tarbes, near Lourdes in the Pyrenees, he had no idea what to do with his life. He toyed with the notion of becoming an engine driver, and then applied to be a machine operator in the local armaments factory, but was turned down for both; so, with no real commitment, he went to cookery school for three years.

Pierre's great passion in life was rugby – his first job, in Switzerland at La Voile D'Or, had to fit round his commitments to the Lausanne Rugby Club, where he played at No 8 in the forward line. He came to England in 1971, to work for Albert Roux at the old Gavroche – and in a very short time had worked his way through the hierarchy. Pierre has Albert to thank on two

counts: the first for meeting his French wife, Annie, and the second for the financial backing to open La Tante Claire in 1977.

There is no Tante Claire in the Koffmann family but if any one person influenced Pierre's life and his style of cooking it was his grandmother, Camille – or 'Mammy', as everyone called her. 'She was a very very good cook and because I was in love with her – when you start to cook you start with your heart.'

As a child Pierre spent every holiday he could at his grandparents' 250-acre farm and he remembers the ritual of closing the farmhouse shutters to watch Mammy flaming her pancakes with Armagnac; her legendary bean soup; the evenings he spent with his head in her lap; her hundred ducks which only Pierre could cajole home at dusk; her night vigils waiting for a stray free-range hen to come home – even if it did ultimately end up as a Poule au Pot. When anyone in the village caught a hare they would bring it to Mammy to cook – always in red wine with a knob of chocolate for extra colour and flavour. A variation of this last dish, using pigeon instead of hare, is one of the dishes Pierre made famous on his menu. But Mammy's Poule au Pot, which takes more than five hours to cook, he reserves for family lunches.

This French bourgeois style is the clue to Pierre's cooking. It has been described as 'brave, working in areas which are frightening to contemplate in other hands' – marrying potentially very strong tastes like the pigeon with chocolate, or sweetbreads with ginger, or the pig's trotters stuffed with sweetbreads which Clement Freud described as 'as delicate a job as knitting a vest of stinging nettles'. Pierre wanted both sweetbreads and pig's trotters on his menu but realized this would reduce the customer's choices except for those who loved offal, so he decided instead to combine the two ingredients in one dish. He is not afraid to serve very simple dishes on his menu – like Terrine de Poireaux aux Truffes, which is simply a dish of steamed leeks which have been cooled under weights to make a terrine, served with a truffle sauce.

Pierre believes that cookery books are all the same and never consults them – and if he had his way he would run a restaurant without a menu, cooking instead what had inspired him that morning. He has compromised that ideal by keeping his à la carte menu for at least six months, while changing his lunch menu daily.

It is well known that plagiarism is common in the competitive world of haute cuisine, but Pierre prides himself that his dishes really are original. This desire to be unique extends to cars too. His Masarati Beta Turbo, as far as he knows, was the first to be seen on England's roads. Now that there are six of them he is looking around for something new.

Pierre has little involvement with other chefs; he is very much an outsider who just gets on with his job, dissociating himself from the politicking and intrigues of his profession. He dislikes high-minded talk about food, and was irritated when cooking was declared an art form by the Société des Beaux Arts in 1984. 'It is quite stupid. Cooking is not an art. My mecha-

nic who looks after my car would you call him an artist because he had done well his job? No.'

The simplicity of Pierre and Annie's lives may be threatened by the recent refurbishment of La Tante Claire. With a bigger kitchen and restaurant they have put themselves on the demanding glory-road towards a third star in the Michelin. They both know people will expect the best cutlery, crockery, linen and cloakrooms – all, in their thinking, complete irrelevancies compared to the quality of food served. As Pierre puts it, 'I just hope I get three stars for my food and not for my new toilets.'

The commitment that great cooks have to give their work continues to amaze me. Pierre finds that 'the kitchen is like a mistress except that it takes up more time'. He shares his kitchen with only three other chefs – and prefers men working with him: 'Women don't have the strength and stamina for fifteen hours in the kitchen.' But he is changing his views following a season with Lucy, an English girl whose sheer obstinancy got her a job.

Nevertheless Pierre's French chauvinism remains in tact. Most of his ingredients, except for beef and lamb, he gets from France. He simply does not trust British suppliers or British produce: 'Leave the French to cook and let the English play cricket.'

When he eats out Pierre chooses Chinese rather than French food because it is less easy to criticize; but he is most happy at home with French friends eating his favourite dish of all – bouillabaisse served with bread which he has baked in his own bread oven in the garden of his home. Of bread he talks lyrically: 'You are dealing with something alive – if you press too hard you kill it. You can feel its life on your skin.' It is ironic that a potentially three-star chef would willingly trade his position with a baker, but that would make Pierre Koffmann extraordinarily happy.

**Albert and Michel Roux** *Côtes d'Agneau à l'Estragon (page 88)*

**Albert and Michel Roux**
*Foie de Veau aux Mangues (page 85)*

**Albert and Michel Roux**   *Rognons de Veau à l'Aigre-Doux  (page 87)*

## Entrecôte aux Echalottes

### Entrecôte with Shallots

| SERVES 4 |
|---|
| 4 entrecôtes about 175 g/6 oz in weight |
| salt |
| pepper |
| 2 tbsp vegetable oil |
| 50 g/2 oz butter |
| 100 g/4 oz chopped shallots |

1. Season the entrecôtes and fry to your taste in the oil.
2. When cooked, remove them to a warm plate and sprinkle with the raw but finely chopped shallots. Top with the butter and cover with another warm plate.
3. Leave to rest for 5 minutes in a warm place before eating.

## Le Foie de Veau au Citron Vert

### Calves' Liver with Lime

| SERVES 4 |
|---|
| 4 slices calves' liver |
| 2 tbsp vegetable oil |
| 2 shallots, chopped |
| 1 tsp sugar |
| 25 ml/1 fl oz vinegar |
| 85 ml/3 fl oz veal stock |
| knob of butter |
| 1 lime, segmented |

1. Fry the liver in the oil on both sides until pink. Remove and keep warm.
2. Discard excess fat from the frying pan, add the shallots and cook gently until soft. Add the sugar and cook until a light gold colour.
3. Add the vinegar and let it reduce completely, then add the veal stock. Heat through, then gradually work in the butter to finish the sauce.
4. Arrange the liver on a serving plate and pour the sauce on top. Garnish with lime.

## Ris de Veau aux Amandes

### Sweetbreads with Almonds

| SERVES 4 |
|---|
| 4 calf sweetbreads |
| salt |
| pepper |
| 2 tbsp vegetable oil |
| 1 onion, chopped |
| 50 g/2 oz butter |
| approx 150 ml/¼ pt port |
| 200 ml/7 fl oz chicken stock |
| 250 ml/8 fl oz double cream |
| juice of ½ lemon |
| 100 g/4 oz sliced almonds, toasted |

1. Clean the sweetbreads, season and then sauté them to seal in the oil before cooking in a 200°C/400°F/Gas Mark 6 oven for 12 minutes.
2. Remove to a side dish. Drain any fat from the pan, add the onion, with the butter, and sweat until soft. Deglaze by stirring in the port and boil until reduced by half.
3. Add the chicken stock and reduce by three-quarters.
5. Add the cream and lemon juice and cook for a few minutes. Pass the sauce through a sieve.
6. Arrange the sweetbreads on a serving dish and pour the sauce on top. Sprinkle with the toasted almonds.

Spinach goes well with this dish.

## Pieds de Cochon aux Morilles

### Pig's Trotters with Morel Mushrooms

| SERVES 4 |
| --- |
| 4 pig's trotters (back legs which have been boned) |
| 100 g/4 oz carrots, cubed |
| 100 g/4 oz onions, cubed |
| 150 ml/¼ pt white wine |
| 1 tbsp port |
| 120 ml/4 fl oz veal stock |
| 225 g/8 oz calf sweetbreads, blanched and chopped |
| 20 dried morel mushrooms, soaked in water |
| 1 small onion, chopped |
| 75 g/3 oz butter |
| 1 breast of chicken, cubed |
| 1 egg white |
| 200 ml/7 fl oz double cream |
| salt |
| pepper |

**1.** Braise the trotters with the carrots, onions, wine, port and veal stock in a slow oven (160°C/325°F/Gas Mark 3) for 3 hours.

**2.** Fry the sweetbreads in 65 g/2½ oz butter for 5 minutes, add the morels and onion and cook for another 5 minutes. Leave to cool.

**3.** Purée the chicken breast with the egg white and double cream, and season. Combine with the sweetbread mixture to make the stuffing.

**4.** Remove the trotters from the oven, keeping the liquid but discarding the vegetables. Put the trotters wide open on tin foil and allow to cool.

**5.** Stuff them with the chicken preparation and roll in foil. Chill for at least 2 hours.

**6.** Cook with very little water in a casserole dish in a 220°C/425°F/Gas Mark 7 oven for 15 minutes.

**7.** When cooked, remove the trotters. Add the stock saved earlier, reduce by half and add a knob of butter. Pour over the trotters and serve.

## Chartreuse D'Agneau au Persil

### Lamb Chartreuse with Parsley

| SERVES 4 |
| --- |
| 4 fillets of lamb |
| 2 carrots, finely sliced lengthwise |
| 2 courgettes, finely sliced lengthwise |
| 450 g/1 lb fresh parsley leaves |
| 2 shallots, chopped |
| 85 ml/3 fl oz white wine vinegar |
| 200 ml/7 fl oz chicken stock |
| 100 g/4 oz butter, cubed |
| 100 ml/3½ fl oz double cream |
| salt |
| pepper |

**1.** Cook the carrots and the courgettes separately in salted water. Drain.

**2.** Cook the parsley in salted water until tender then press it hard to remove all the water.

**3.** Line 4 buttered flowerpot-shaped moulds (*darioles*) with the carrots and courgettes. Leave to one side.

**4.** Cook the lamb in a roasting pan in the oven at 240°C/475°F/Gas Mark 9 for about 10 minutes or to your taste.

**5.** While the lamb is cooking, warm the cream in a pan and then add the parsley and season.

**6.** Place the creamed parsley in the moulds, pressing it well in, and then turn out each mould on to a serving plate.

**7.** When the lamb is cooked, remove it to a side dish. Drain excess fat from the pan, add the shallots and sweat them until soft.

**8.** Deglaze with the vinegar and reduce by half. Add the chicken stock and again reduce by half.

**9.** Beat in the butter off the heat.

**10.** Slice the fillets of lamb, arrange around the parsley moulds and pour over the sauce.

**Peter Kromberg** *Top, Ragoût d'Artichauts aux Coriandres (page 93); bottom left, Ragoût d'Aubergines aux Senteurs de Basilic (page 93); bottom right, Poireaux Braisés Ma Façon (page 96)*

**Peter Kromberg** *Top, Crottin de Chavignol Grillé avec Salade Mesclun (page 92); bottom, Soufflé aux Brocolis avec Tapenade (page 96)*

# Poularde Henri IV or Poule au Pot

### Henri IV's Chicken or Chicken in the Pot

Served with farcidure, stuffed cabbage and cream sauce.

| |
|---|
| **1 large hen, cleaned** |
| **4 carrots, chopped** |
| **4 leeks, chopped** |
| **4 turnips, chopped** |
| **4 onions, chopped** |
| **2–3 cloves of garlic to taste, mashed** |
| **1 clove, chopped** |
| **bouquet garni** |
| **salt** |
| **pepper** |

*For the stuffing*

| |
|---|
| **1 large slice Bayonne ham, chopped** |
| **10 slices white bread (crusts removed), soaked in milk and pressed dry** |
| **hen's liver, sautéed in butter and chopped** |
| **2 eggs** |
| **salt** |
| **pepper** |
| **4 cloves of garlic, mashed** |
| **4 shallots, chopped** |
| **1 piece of cinnamon bark** |

**1.** Clean the hen and then mix all the stuffing ingredients together in a food processor and stuff the hen. Sew the hen firmly at each end.
**2.** Put the stuffed hen into a very large pot with the vegetables, garlic, clove, bouquet garni, salt and pepper, and cover with water. Cook for at least 2 hours – simmering gently. (Giblets including feet can be cooked with the chicken.) If you prefer crispier vegetables only add them when you have 15 minutes' cooking time left.

### Farcidure

A dumpling to be served with the Poule au Pot.

| |
|---|
| **25 g/1 oz yeast** |
| **pinch of salt** |
| **pinch of sugar** |
| **675 g/1½ lb flour** |
| **100 g/4 oz butter** |
| **3 eggs** |

**1.** Mix the yeast in a little warm water, following the instructions on the packet, and add salt and sugar.
**2.** Mix the flour, butter and eggs with the yeast in a food processor.
**3.** Roll the mixture into a ball and leave to rise for a few hours under a cloth.
**4.** An hour before you are ready to eat, put the farcidure to cook in the pot with the hen, covering it with a lid. Cook for ½ hour on one side and then turn and cook for ½ hour on the other side.

### Chou Farci

Stuffed Cabbage – an optional addition to the basic Poule au Pot.

| |
|---|
| **1 large green cabbage** |

*For the stuffing*

| |
|---|
| **225 g/8 oz lean pork, cut in pieces and browned** |
| **225 g/8 oz lean pork back fat, cut in pieces and browned** |
| **2 eggs** |
| **2 tsp mixed fresh herbs or 1 tsp dried** |
| **1–2 cloves of garlic, chopped (optional)** |
| **salt** |
| **pepper** |
| **handful of breadcrumbs** |

1. Clean the green cabbage and blanch it in boiling salted water for 8 minutes.
2. Mix the stuffing ingredients.
3. Rinse the cabbage in cold water, drain it and remove the large outer leaves.
4. Remove the ribbed stem from these leaves and spread the leaves out flat on a thin damp teatowel.
5. Put some stuffing into the centre of the cabbage leaves – and then place the cabbage heart on to the stuffing before covering with more stuffing and then cabbage leaves so that the cabbage shape is re-formed. Pull the ends of the cloth together and tie firmly.
6. Poach the cabbage in the cooking pot with the hen ½ hour after cooking has started.

### Sauce Crème

| |
|---|
| **100 ml/4 fl oz chicken stock** |
| **200 ml/7 fl oz béchamel sauce** |
| **50 g/2 oz butter** |
| **4 tbsp cream** |

1. Add the chicken stock to the béchamel sauce and cook over a low heat until hot.
2. Remove from the heat and stir in the butter and cream.
3. Strain the sauce before serving.

**To serve**
When all the ingredients are cooked, remove the vegetables, cabbage, farcidure and hen from the pot and drain them. Strain the stock and serve at the beginning of the meal as a soup.

Cut the hen and arrange it on the dish with vegetables around it. Cut the stuffed cabbage and arrange it on the dish. Cut the farcidure and serve as bread. Serve the cream sauce with the dishes.

*Bon appetit.*

# *Fricassée de Volaille aux Écrevisses*

*Chicken Fricassee with Crayfish*

| SERVES 4 |
|---|
| **1 chicken (2 kg/4½ lb)** |
| **12 large freshwater crayfish** |
| **100 g/4 oz butter** |
| **600 ml/1 pt double cream** |

| *For the court-bouillon* |
|---|
| **1 litre/1¾ pt water** |
| **250 ml/8 fl oz white wine** |
| **½ onion, chopped** |
| **1 carrot, chopped** |
| **1 leek, chopped** |
| **½ stick celery, chopped** |
| **salt** |
| **pepper** |
| **cayenne pepper** |
| **bouquet garni** |

1. Combine the ingredients for the court-bouillon and cook the crayfish in this for 5 minutes.
2. Cut the chicken in 8 pieces. Sauté it in the butter, then cook, covered, in a 200°C/400°F/Gas Mark 6 oven for 15 minutes.
3. Remove the cooked crayfish from their shells, keeping 4 heads back for decoration. Add the rest of the shells to the chicken pan when the chicken is half-cooked.
4. When the chicken is cooked, remove it to a side plate.
5. Remove any fat from the pan, add the cream, and boil until reduced by half. Pour the sauce through a sieve and then add the crayfish.
6. Arrange the chicken on a warm plate, pour the sauce over it and decorate with the crayfish heads.

## *Lapereau Farci aux Foie Gras, Artichauts et Truffe*

*Rabbit Stuffed with Foie Gras, Artichokes and Truffle*

SERVES 4

| |
|---|
| 1 rabbit, skinned and cleaned with rib bones removed, or 2 small rabbits, skinned and cleaned |
| 225 g/8 oz fresh foie gras |
| 1 truffle |
| 2 hearts of artichokes, cooked |
| 2 tbsp vegetable oil |
| 25 ml/1 fl oz Armagnac |
| 200 ml/7 fl oz chicken stock |
| knob of butter |

**1.** Cut the fresh foie gras, truffle and artichoke heart into cubes, and mix. Stuff the inside of the rabbit with the mixture.
**2.** Sew the rabbit's belly and roast it in the oil in the oven at 220°C/425°F/Gas Mark 7 for 20–30 minutes.
**3.** When cooked, remove the rabbit from the pan and keep warm.
**4.** Pour off the fat and add the Armagnac and chicken stock. Reduce the liquid until it coats the back of a spoon, then add the butter.
**5.** Slice the rabbit, arrange on a serving plate and pour over the sauce.

## *Le Pigeonneau Rôti au Vinaigre de Framboises et au Chocolat Amer*

*Roast Pigeon with Raspberry Vinegar and Bitter Chocolate*

SERVES 4

| |
|---|
| 4 pigeons (corn-fed) |
| salt |
| pepper |
| 2 tbsp vegetable oil |
| 2 tsp finely chopped shallot |
| 50 ml/2 fl oz raspberry vinegar |
| approx 150 ml/¼ pt red wine |
| 300 ml/½ pt veal stock |
| 4 cubes bitter chocolate |
| knob of butter |

**1.** Season the pigeons and sauté them in the oil for 10–15 minutes (the flesh should be pink). When cooked, remove them and place on a plate.
**2.** Discard excess fat from the pan, add the shallot and let it sweat until soft.
**3.** Deglaze by stirring in the vinegar and reduce completely by boiling.
**4.** Add the wine and reduce until a quarter of the mixture is left.
**5.** Add the veal stock and the chocolate. When the chocolate has melted add a knob of butter.
**6.** Carve the pigeons, arrange on a plate and serve with the sauce poured over the top.

# Albert & Michel Roux
## on Meat

'A day without cooking is like a day without sunshine. It's a medicine which I need. I need the stove. I need my pans and I need the atmosphere of my kitchen.' Albert Roux, small, very dark, almost impish-looking, has an extraordinary love of cooking – and his brother Michel is equally dedicated: 'I can't live without thinking about food really. I can't get it out of my system.'

The brothers' love affair with food was nurtured at home (their parents ran a charcuterie). Mealtimes were sacrosanct – dinner was always at six, and a time for family discussion. A respect for food and its preparation was instilled in them – though Michel believes that love of food is a gift and cannot be taught.

As money was scarce (the family lived modestly in the village of Charolles, near Macon), meals in the Roux household were based on cheap ingredients. For example, a favourite dish was a simple casserole of heart and carrots. No cream was added, just a dash of white wine and a sprig of parsley. The boys were encouraged to experiment with cooking in their mother's kitchen, but their apprenticeship as pastry-cooks added craft and a respect for precision in cooking to their early enthusiasm. Neither is

willing to say who is the better cook: Albert's brioches and croissants are perfection, while Michel's cakes and desserts are supreme. Both brothers have earned three Michelin stars, Michel at the Waterside Inn at Bray and Albert at Le Gavroche in Mayfair.

Albert can bring a menu to life as he describes the dishes: 'Foie gras from a little man I know in Landes – duck rather than goose liver because I think there's more flavour – in a little Jurasson (that's a sweet white wine from the Jura mountains), or perhaps a little rascasse – a highly flavoured fish from the Mediterranean. And with him we have freshwater crayfish with a light sauce of cucumber.' Albert describes his cuisine as 'rich but light. When you have finished your meal you are quite ready to have another. Very rich in calorie but light and when you achieve that you are pretty near perfection.'

Good ingredients and seasonal produce of quality are, of course, essential: their strawberries, raspberries, salmon and beef are British, but almost everything else comes from Rungis, the enormous market just outside Paris. Albert and Michel trained Dominic Roussel, an employee of ten years' standing, to have an eye for the market. They bought him a lorry and now,

# Albert and Michel Roux on Meat

once a week, it returns to London from Paris laden with every kind of poultry, fish, vegetables, fruit and cheese. But Albert cannot resist a trip himself at least once a month.

Wherever he goes, whether to a cheap market canteen for mussels in sauce or to a friend's Hôtellerie du Bas at Barbizon near Fontainebleau for delicate mousselines, Albert will take notes, so that some day he will create his own version of the dishes he has enjoyed.

Michel shares his constant interest. Even on a seaside holiday his first pleasure will be to find the market, and perhaps cook for an hour or two. Only then will he bask in the sea and sun. The desire to experiment is unending in both men. Albert can arrive at Le Gavroche, having seen fresh rhubarb on a vegetable stall on his way there, and (remembering the scallops in his fridge) will create a gratin of rhubarb and scallops, which proves delicious.

Neither brother is an onlooker in the kitchen. They have to cook, but only in their own way. Albert refuses to well-cook his meat, or to use bay leaves ('bad for the heart, you could kill your mother-in-law with them') and garlic and pepper are only used sparingly because they can overpower natural flavours. Michel likes to season meat before he cooks it, whereas Albert prefers to wait until the juices are running before he adds salt, to stop a crust forming on the meat. Sauces are rarely stirred, for both Michel and Albert prefer to *vanne*, or make waves, with the saucepan.

Albert firmly believes he can tell whether an apprentice will have any flair for cooking by the way he chops parsley or fries an egg – which should take three to four minutes to cook, and should never stick to the pan.

One of Albert's apprentices, Susie Elen, comments, 'Albert is a worker. He hasn't changed because he has made money. And he likes to see people get on. He says we owe it to our trade to

try.' But although they like to pass on their own philosophy and standards, the brothers are no mere philanthropists. The Waterside Inn can take £30,000 during Ascot week alone.

Michel's most admired inspiration, Marie-Antoine Carême, also moved from frugality to riches. A child of a poor family, with upwards of seventeen siblings often quoted, he found work as a kitchen boy and taught himself to read and write. By the age of 40 he had cooked for the French court and written eight classic cookery books. His dictum was 'the chef who is a man of routine lacks courage; his life drops away in mediocrity'. Michel unquestionably follows his example. Albert's mentor is Edward Nignon, who also began his career as a pastry-cook. He would say 'he who gets the key of the citrus and all acidy fruit will have the key to heaven as far as cooking is concerned', a piece of advice which Albert has kept firmly in mind.

For a dish to become a classic it must be recognized by the Academie Culinaire (an exclusive French organization which cooks are invited to join and for which they must be endorsed by at least two existing members). Albert would choose to be remembered by a cassoulet of lamb, goose, sausage, garlic and beans. Michel's dish is less simple: a Blanquette de Veau à l'Ancienne.

According to Paul Bocuse, a great chef is one who finds two new dishes in a lifetime. Already Michel regards as a classic his dish of Feuilleté d'Huitres au Vinaigre de Framboise and there is no doubt the brothers will find the other three.

Although most of the dishes they serve have rich ingredients and exotic names, the brothers' tastes are more simple. Albert's last meal on earth would certainly not be a classic, but instead 'a little bit of skirt, preferably rump skirt with nice crispy chips'. For Michel, the choice is easy: Heart and Carrots, the way his mother used to make it.

# Poulet Bresse en Vessie

### *Chicken in a Vest*

SERVES 4

| |
|---|
| 1 chicken (1–1½ kg/2½–3 lb) |
| 100 g/4 oz foie gras |
| salt |
| pepper |
| 2 truffles and their juice |
| 150 ml/¼ pt port |
| 150 ml/¼ pt brandy |
| 2 tbsp double cream |
| knob of butter |

*For the garnish*

| |
|---|
| 4 small carrots, cut in thin pieces |
| 4 small leeks, cut in thin pieces |
| 300 ml/½ pt chicken stock |
| 225 g/8 oz ravioli |

1. Trim and clean the chicken. Slice the foie gras and season it with salt and pepper.
2. Slice the truffles, and pack the foie gras and the truffles beneath the skin of the chicken next to the breast.
3. Place the chicken in either a pig's bladder, if available (previously soaked in vinegar to clean and soften it), or a roasting bag, and pour over the port and brandy. Add salt and pepper to taste. Seal the bag tightly and cook gently in a large pan of boiling water for 1½ hours.
4. Remove the chicken from the saucepan and break open the bag, releasing the juices into a clean saucepan. Carve the chicken into 4 pieces.
5. Using the carcase as a presentation base, rebuild the chicken into shape on the serving dish, and keep warm.
7. To make the garnish, poach the carrots and leeks in the chicken stock with the ravioli until cooked. Drain and keep warm.
8. Add the truffle juice and the cream to the juices from the chicken, and reduce by boiling until thickened. Adjust the seasoning to taste.
9. Add a knob of butter to the sauce, stirring until melted, to make it shiny, then pour it over the chicken.
10. Decorate the dish with the prepared vegetable and ravioli garnish.

# Foie de Veau aux Mangues

### *Calf Liver with Mangoes*

SERVES 4

| |
|---|
| 4 slices calves' liver (approx 185 g/6½ oz each) |
| 2 well-ripened mangoes, thinly sliced |
| 1 tbsp flour |
| 100 g/4 oz butter |
| 25 g/1 oz shallots |
| 200 ml/7 fl oz port or Madeira |
| 150 ml/¼ pt veal stock (optional) |
| salt |
| ground pepper |
| 1 bunch of cress |

1. Cut the liver into thin slices. Coat them very lightly on both sides with the flour.
2. Cook in a very hot frying pan with half the butter for a few minutes on each side. Leave on a plate or serving dish in a hot place.
3. Sauté the chopped shallots in the same frying pan, then mix in the port or Madeira and boil until reduced by half.
4. Add the stock or a little water and cook for a few minutes.
5. Add the remaining butter and season to taste.
6. Pour the sauce over the liver and arrange the sliced mangoes around it. Garnish with cress and serve at once.

# Queue de Boeuf aux Echalottes

*Oxtail Garnished with Shallots*

SERVES 8

| |
|---|
| 1.9 kg/4½ lb large oxtails |
| 675 g/1½ lb large onions |
| 150 g/5 oz celery |
| 900 g/2 lb medium-sized carrots |
| dried rind of 2 oranges (optional) |
| 3 cloves |
| 1 tbsp peppercorns |
| bouquet garni |
| 8 large firm mushrooms (separate stems from caps) |
| 65 g/2½ oz garlic |
| 2 litres/3½ pt red wine, preferably Burgundy |
| 150 ml/¼ pt olive oil |
| table salt |
| 2 tbsp flour |
| 450 ml/¾ pt veal stock |
| 2 or 3 pieces of pork rind (optional) |
| 40 medium-sized shallots |
| 200 g/8 oz coarse salt |
| 350 g/12 oz medium-sized courgettes |
| 90 g/3½ oz butter |
| 2 sprigs of parsley |

**1.** At least 26 hours before they are required for cooking, put the oxtails to soak in cold water for a few hours.

**2.** With a knife remove the excess fat if necessary. Cut into pieces at each joint. Place in an earthenware pot.

**3.** Peel the onions, celery and one-third of the carrots. Wash and cut into big pieces. Add to the oxtails, along with the orange rind, cloves, ground peppercorns, bouquet garni, washed mushroom stems and garlic (not skinned). Add all the wine and half the olive oil.

**4.** Cover with greaseproof paper and leave to marinate for 24 hours in the refrigerator.

**5.** Set the oven to 180°C/350°F/Gas Mark 4.

**6.** Strain all the marinade ingredients through a large strainer. Put the resulting liquid on to boil for a few minutes. Keep it hot.

**7.** Cook all the vegetables and flavourings from the marinade in the remaining olive oil in a braising/stewing pan over a brisk heat for 6–8 minutes.

**8.** Remove excess liquid from the oxtails with kitchen roll and salt lightly. Heat them with a little more olive oil in a frying pan until coated on all sides.

**9.** Put the flour on to a pie dish and place in the oven until it turns a nut-brown colour. Add the oxtails and stir with a spatula. Then place them in the braising pan on the bed of vegetables.

**10.** Add the wine from the marinade, stock and approximately 1 litre/1¾ pt water.

**11.** Put the pork rind on top and bring to the boil. Cover: the vessel should be airtight. Place in the oven for 2½ hours.

**12.** For the garnish, place the whole shallots on a bed of coarse salt on a baking tray, so that they do not touch each other. Cook at 200°C/400°F/Gas Mark 6 for about 14 minutes.

**13.** Check to see if cooked by piercing with the point of a knife. Remove skins. Leave at room temperature.

**14.** Peel the rest of the carrots and cut lengthwise in 3-mm/⅛-in slices. Cook for 3 minutes in boiling salted water. Leave to cool.

**15.** Cut off the ends of the courgettes and cut lengthwise into 3-mm/⅛-in slices. Cook for 1 minute in boiling salted water, then leave to cool. Add to the carrots.

**16.** Cut the mushrooms heads crosswise in 3-mm/⅛-in slices. Set aside with the carrots and courgettes.

**17.** When the oxtails are cooked, lift them out gently and place on a deep serving dish. Cover and keep hot.

**18.** Strain the liquid into a shallow frying pan. Remove the fat, then reduce in volume by two-thirds over a brisk heat, skimming the fat as often as necessary.

**19.** Add all the butter in small pieces over a gentle heat: the liquid should be semi-syrupy.

**20.** Add all the vegetable garnishes and season. Bring to the boil and pour over the oxtails. Sprinkle with chopped parsley and serve at once.

# Rognons de Veau à l'Aigre-Doux

### Sweet and Sour Veal Kidneys

Light, fruity, but slightly sour because of the bilberries, this dish takes little time to prepare but is very elegant and satisfying.

SERVES 4

| |
|---|
| 2 kidneys, approx 450 g/1 lb, without fat and veins |
| 1 orange |
| 2 lemons |
| 4 tbsp port |
| 40 g/1½ oz caster sugar |
| 100 g/4 oz bilberries |
| 1 tbsp white wine vinegar |
| 150 ml/¼ pt veal stock |
| 50 g/2 oz clarified butter |
| 1 tsp dry English mustard |
| salt |
| pepper |
| 25 g/1 oz butter |

**1.** Peel the orange and lemons very finely, shred the peel in thin strips, and blanch for a few moments in boiling water. Set aside to cool.

**2.** Remove the pith from the orange, cut into quarters and reserve. Squeeze the juice from the lemon and reserve also.

**3.** Heat the port in a small saucepan with a quarter (nearly 1 tbsp) of the sugar. When the liquid is boiling and the sugar has dissolved, add the bilberries and cook for 1 minute. Keep warm.

**4.** Heat the rest of the sugar with the vinegar in another small saucepan until caramelized. Remove from the heat and add the lemon juice.

**5.** Return to the heat, add the orange quarters and the stock, and cook gently for about 15 minutes until the sauce is of a syrupy consistency. Strain the sauce and keep it hot.

**6.** Cut the kidneys into thin strips. Heat the clarified butter in a frying pan until bubbling and fry the kidneys lightly, for no more than 1 minute. They must be underdone and golden in colour. Remove the kidneys from the pan and pour off the butter.

**7.** Pour the port liquid from the bilberries into the pan, reserving the berries, and heat up again quickly. Boil until reduced by half, then add the syrupy sauce.

**8.** Bring back to the boil, add the kidneys, bilberries and the mustard, which has been mixed with ½ tsp water.

**9.** Season to taste, and add the butter to shine the sauce. Do not let the sauce boil again at this point, or the kidneys will become hard.

**10.** Pour the kidneys and their sauce into a deep serving dish, sprinkle over the grated, prepared rinds of orange and lemon, and serve at once.

Buttered pasta or apple purée goes well with this dish.

## Côtes d'Agneau à l'Estragon

*Lamb Chops with Tarragon*

| SERVES 4 |
|---|
| rack of lamb (allow 2 chops per persons) |
| 50 g/2 oz butter |
| salt |
| 50 g/2 oz shallots, finely chopped |
| scant 2 tbsp tarragon vinegar |
| 150 ml/¼ pt double cream |
| sprigs of fresh tarragon, to garnish |

**1.** Separate the chops from the bones, or ask your butcher to prepare them for you. Trim off most of the fat, leaving only the eye of the meat on the bone.

**2.** Using half the butter, sauté the chops in a heavy frying pan over a high heat (adding a little salt as the meat seals) until they are brown outside but pink-centred. Set aside on a serving plate and keep warm.

**3.** Add the shallots to the butter in the pan, and toss for a few seconds until just transparent.

**4.** Add the vinegar – there may be a few flames as the fumes burn off.

**5.** Slowly pour in the cream, and *vanne*, or make waves, with the pan, rolling the cream backwards and forwards through the pan juices until amalgamated.

**6.** Add the remainder of the butter to make the sauce smooth and shiny, moving the pan gently again as the butter melts into the sauce.

**7.** Check the seasoning and pour the sauce over the chops. Garnish with sprigs of fresh tarragon.

## Langues d'Agneau au Coulis de Tomates

*Lambs' Tongues with Tomato Coulis*

| SERVES 4 |
|---|
| 12 lambs' tongues |
| 2 carrots |
| 1 small onion |
| 1 clove |
| bouquet garni |
| 50 g/2 oz butter |
| 25 g/1 oz finely chopped shallot |
| 1 small clove of garlic, crushed |
| 1 sprig of thyme, crumbled |
| 900 g/2 lb well-ripened tomatoes, cut in large pieces |
| salt |
| ground pepper |
| pinch of sugar (optional) |
| 1 sprig of parsley, chopped, to garnish |

**1.** Soak the tongues in cold water for 1 hour, then blanch in boiling water for 10 minutes. Cool. Drain, dry, and cut lengthwise.

**2.** Place in a saucepan with 1 carrot, the onion, clove and bouquet garni, and cover with cold water. Bring to the boil, then simmer for approximately 2 hours.

**3.** Test whether the tongues are cooked by pricking with a knife: they should be soft and the juices should run clear. Keep hot.

**4.** Heat half the butter in a pan and add the shallot, garlic, thyme and finally the tomatoes. Cook gently, stirring from time to time, for 45 minutes.

**5.** Whisk in the remaining butter and season to taste with salt and pepper. (Add a pinch of sugar if the sauce is slightly acid.)

**6.** Pour the tomato sauce into a serving dish. Arrange the tongues, skinned and cut lengthwise, on top and garnish with parsley.

## Ris de Veau au Porto et à la Crème

*Calf Sweetbreads with Port and Cream*

SERVES 4

| |
|---|
| 4 rounded calf sweetbreads, not prepared (approx 225 g/8 oz each) |
| 50 g/2 oz butter |
| 200 ml/7 fl oz Ruby port |
| 200 ml/7 fl oz double cream |
| 130 ml/scant ¼ pt veal stock (optional) |
| salt |
| ground pepper |

**1.** Clean the sweetbreads in cold running water, then blanch in boiling water for a few minutes and cool.

**2.** Trim and remove the thickest skins. Place the sweetbreads between two sheets of kitchen paper under light pressure (cover with wooden board and add a weight of 675 g/1½ lb maximum). Leave in a cool place until flattened.

**3.** Heat the butter in a frying pan and add the sweetbreads. Cook until a light golden colour – about 5 minutes on each side. Keep on a plate or serving dish in a hot place.

**4.** Add the port to the frying pan, and reduce by half.

**5.** Add the cream, then the stock, and cook gently for 5 minutes.

**6.** Season to taste with salt and pepper. Strain the sauce straight on to the sweetbreads, and serve at once.

Broccoli or pilaf rice go well with this dish.

## Coeur de Veau aux Carottes

*Heart and Carrots*

SERVES 4

| |
|---|
| 2 veal hearts or 6 lamb hearts (veal are better) |
| 100 g/4 oz butter |
| 900 g/2 lb small new carrots, scraped |
| 1 large onion, finely chopped |
| bouquet garni |
| 1 clove of garlic, crushed |
| 150 ml/¼ pt dry white wine |
| 4 tbsp water |
| salt |
| pepper |
| 1 sprig of parsley, chopped |

**1.** Place the hearts in a bowl under cold running water for about 2 hours to clean them. Drain, trim off the fat and dry well, then seal in half the butter in a heavy casserole.

**2.** Add the whole carrots, tossing them gently until coated in butter, then add the onion and cook until transparent.

**3.** Add the bouquet garni and crushed garlic, and then pour in the white wine.

**4.** Cover and place in a 180°C/350°F/Gas Mark 4 oven for 25–30 minutes for the lamb hearts, or 45 minutes for the veal. When tender, remove the hearts and vegetables, and keep warm.

**5.** Over a gentle heat, add the water and the remainder of the butter to the juice in the pan. Season with salt and freshly ground pepper. Heat until well amalgamated, then pour the juice through a fine sieve.

**6.** If using veal hearts, keep the sauce warm and cut the hearts into slices. Leave the lamb hearts whole.

**7.** Place the hearts on a serving dish and pour the sauce over them. Garnish with a little freshly chopped parsley.

# Peter Kromberg
## on
## Vegetables

Peter Kromberg will always remember his first day as a cook. The place was the Duisberger Hof near Dusseldorf. The date was 13 April 1955. His job to scale, clean and fillet twelve large cod. It took him six hours. He was only fourteen.

Thirty years later Peter is executive chef at the Inter-Continental Hotel in London, and its restaurant, Le Soufflé, has been credited with a Michelin star – a rare achievement for a hotel serving 10 000 meals a week.

Peter's father was a master pâtissier who died when Peter was only ten weeks old. Nevertheless Kromberg Senior's reputation lived on at the hotel where he had worked – the same hotel where Peter began his apprenticeship. He wanted to emulate his father, but not by becoming a pâtissier: 'I used to watch the local pâtissier work and his large scales put me off – it looked too much like chemistry.' During his apprenticeship Peter worked 'like a robot because I did what people asked me to do. Only when I was about 23 did I begin to question, to evaluate and to think for myself.' After training in Athens, Switzerland and Bangkok, Peter joined the Inter-Continental Hotel Group in 1966 and has been executive chef at the London

Inter-Continental since it opened in 1975.

His weekly grocery order is enormous – 10 000 oranges, 550 lb of tomatoes, 700 lb of onions and a ton of potatoes. The number of eggs used can only be guessed at, as he serves at least 350 soufflés a week in the restaurant, let alone the lunch and evening banquets, where as many as 400 will be cooked at a time. Soufflés apart, Peter finds it difficult to describe his cooking. 'It's nothing to do with nouvelle cuisine and it's not really classical either. The basics are classical but then we do what we feel is right.' Ideas come to Peter when a supplier phones him up offering something special like crayfish or white aubergine or tiny cauliflowers. He rarely consults books but sits with his *sous chef* exchanging ideas with culinary confidence, knowing exactly what will marry with what to produce a good but different result. Then, with less confidence in his typing, Peter taps out with one finger the menu for the following week.

It is one thing to create a menu but Peter then has to delegate his style of cooking to his 50-strong kitchen brigade. Every Saturday he has tastings where new dishes are cooked and adjusted to suit his palate. Although he favours generous portions he cannot bear to see an overcrowded plate or unrelieved colours. Herb garnishes are very important, but only one precise position will do on the plate. Despite that, his presentation is unpretentious and he balks at eating dishes like the sugared fresh daffodils which were once placed in front of him. When the colour of a nouvelle cuisine sauce seems more important than its taste, Peter believes it is time to draw a halt.

He leads his team in a very democratic way. His calm affable manner percolates through to his staff, and it is certainly one of the most relaxed kitchens I have visited – which doesn't mean Peter isn't demanding. He got angry when a new chef started his shift wearing plimsoles: 'It's not the hygiene, but I can't understand how he can work for maybe twelve hours wearing the cheapest shoes he can find. He can't be talented because he's not thinking enough about himself.' Apart from footwear, there are other ways Peter spots talent. How an apprentice holds a knife will be a clue to his chance as a chef: the thumb, not the finger, should be on top of the knife. How a chef handles produce is another clue. The worst sin is when a lettuce is ripped from its root and most of the leaves end up in the bin; that shows a complete lack of understanding of the value of the product.

Peter is perhaps more interested than most chefs in new talent coming into the profession. He is a member of Club Nine (as are Richard Shepherd, Anton Mosimann and John Huber) and, like them, he is keen to foster talent and promote better training for new chefs. His own comprehensive training has certainly given him the confidence to excel in any section of the kitchen.

Cooking in bulk Peter dismisses as easy: 'You just use bigger pans!' But that is not to denigrate his banqueting skills, which have drawn a lot of bookings away from other large hotels in London. It used to be unusual to eat well at a banquet for 400, but times are surely changing. Now there are very few things Peter cannot or will not serve. He never serves a soufflé as a first course because guests may be late; but when the end of the meal arrives, 400 chocolate soufflés rising in unison and proudly entering the dining room is a common but quite incredible sight.

The hours chefs work never ceases to amaze me, but Peter is one of the few chefs I have met who has put his working life into perspective. His French wife Nicole and his two boys are as important to him as his work, and he makes quite sure that he spends time with them. 'You should be able to balance your life in a way that you do not spend from seven in the morning to twelve o'clock at night sweating in the kitchen and being there very often just for the sake of being there. I have seen too many chefs living the last few years of their life on their own because their families couldn't stand it.'

Although Peter and his restaurant manager eat out at least once a month – 'competition shopping', they call it – to keep pace with what is going on around them, he is just as happy taking his sons to McDonald's. Much to his delight, they are both developing a taste for sauces other than ketchup.

Refreshingly, Peter Kromberg is quite happy with his one Michelin star and doesn't yearn for two or three. Other cooks regard him with total respect: 'Any hotel dining room that receives recognition in the Michelin is a very, very good dining room,' said Nico Ladenis of Peter recently, and all his colleagues recognize that to satisfy all the different customer requirements, to turn your hand to every style of cooking, *and* to do it well, is indeed an impressive achievement.

The satisfaction of the achievement is summed up by Peter: 'What I get out of it at the end of the day is when I look at the dish-wash and the plates come back empty – I think that is the best, the greatest compliment for a chef.'

## Aumônière de Pipérade

*Alms-Purse with Pipérade*

SERVES 6

*For the pancake*

| |
|---|
| 2 eggs |
| 2 heaped tbsp strong flour, sieved |
| 25 g/1 oz melted butter |
| 150 ml/¼ pt milk (approx) |
| salt |
| nutmeg |
| butter, for frying |

*For the filling*

| |
|---|
| 1 red pepper |
| 1 green pepper |
| 25 ml/1 fl oz olive oil |
| 1 clove of garlic, crushed |
| ½ onion, chopped |
| 1 large ripe tomato, peeled and de-seeded |
| 100 g/4 oz diced ham (optional) |
| 6 fresh chives or strips of leeks |

**1.** Make a batter with all the pancake ingredients to the consistency of liquid cream.
**2.** In a heavy iron pan with as little butter as possible, fry 6 very thin pancakes. Let them cool on a drip tray or absorbent paper.
**3.** Meanwhile fry the whole peppers slowly with a little of the oil until the skin starts to peel off.
**4.** Place the peppers in a roasting bag, put into a preheated oven at 180°C/350°F/Gas Mark 4 and leave for 20 minutes.
**5.** Remove the peppers from the bag, peel, remove core and cut in half. Remove all seeds and cut the flesh into 1-cm/½-in squares.
**6.** Heat the remaining oil in a saucepan. Add the garlic and onion and sweat until golden.
**7.** Add the peppers and tomato. Cover with a lid and simmer for approximately 15 minutes. Add seasoning, and ham if required.

**8.** Place small heaps of this mixture in the middle of the pancakes, bring all the edges together at the top and tie like an alms-purse with a long chive or a strip of leek.
**9.** Bake them in a hot oven (220°C/425°F/Gas Mark 7) until crispy, and serve on a dish with the remaining pipérade around.

This dish makes a nice accompaniment to a roast and can be prepared in advance.

## Crottin de Chavignol Grillé avec Salade Mesclun

*Mesclun with Crottin de Chavignol Cheese*

SERVES 6

| |
|---|
| 6 portions Mesclun salad (see note) |
| 3 Crottin de Chavignol cheeses |
| 10 ml/½ fl oz olive oil |
| 1 tsp sweet paprika |
| 6 slices of granary French bread |
| 50 g/2 oz coarsely chopped walnuts |

*For the vinaigrette*

| |
|---|
| 120 ml/4 fl oz red wine vinegar |
| 1 tbsp Dijon mustard |
| 10 ml/½ fl oz hot water |
| salt |
| pepper |
| 200 ml/7 fl oz walnut oil |

*Note:* Mesclun salad (a combination of sorrel, curly endive, oakleaf, chervil, rocket, Parisian lettuce, 'doublefair' endive) is readily available in the summer at top-class greengrocers.

**1.** Wash the salad well and dry it by swinging in cheesecloth or using a salad spinner.
**2.** Prepare the vinaigrette by mixing all ingredients, but add the oil slowly, a little at a time.
**3.** Cut the cheeses in half, spread with olive oil and sprinkle with paprika. Place on toasted

French bread and grill until melting.

**4.** Gently mix the vinaigrette with the salad, taking care not to bruise the fragile leaves, and add the walnuts.

**5.** Arrange on plates and serve with the hot grilled cheeses.

## Ragoût d'Artichauts aux Coriandres

*Mediterranean Artichoke Stew with Fresh Coriander*

| SERVES 6 |
| --- |
| 6 large globe artichokes |
| 1 lemon, cut in half |
| 2 medium-sized carrots, peeled |
| 50 g/2 oz chopped raisins |
| 120 ml/4 fl oz white wine |
| 25 ml/1 fl oz virgin olive oil |
| 2 cloves of garlic, crushed |
| 15 button onions, peeled |
| 15 button mushrooms, washed |
| pinch of saffron |
| 1 large ripe tomato, peeled, de-seeded and diced |
| 15 small new potatoes, peeled |
| 1 bunch of fresh coriander leaves, snipped with scissors |

**1.** Cut off the artichoke leaves. Remove the hairy middle with a spoon. Rub with lemon.

**2.** Cut the carrots into batons 4 cm/1½ in × 1 cm/½ in.

**3.** Soak the raisins in white wine.

**4.** Heat the olive oil in a heavy-bottomed saucepan. Add the garlic and artichokes. Sweat for 5 minutes without colouring, then add the carrots, onions, mushrooms and saffron. Cover and sweat for 5 minutes.

**5.** Add the tomatoes, raisins and wine and bring to the boil. Cook, covered, in a 180°C/

350°F/Gas Mark 4 oven for 20 minutes.

**6.** Add the potatoes and return to the oven until all ingredients are tender. Do not stir because you might break the vegetables.

**7.** Remove from the oven and sprinkle with the snipped coriander leaves.

This dish can be eaten hot or cold. Personally, I prefer it cold in the summer.

## Ragoût d'Aubergines aux Senteurs de Basilic

*Aubergine Ragoût with Basil*

| SERVES 6 |
| --- |
| 4–5 ripe aubergines |
| 120 ml/4 fl oz virgin olive oil |
| 1 medium onion, chopped |
| 2 cloves of garlic, crushed with a little salt |
| 2 ripe tomatoes, peeled, de-seeded and diced |
| 1 bunch of fresh basil (separate leaves from stalks) |
| 2 anchovy fillets |
| sea salt |
| freshly milled black pepper |

**1.** Peel the aubergines and dice into 2.5-cm/1-in chunks.

**2.** Heat the olive oil in a heavy saucepan. Add the onion and garlic and sweat until golden.

**3.** Add the aubergines, tomatoes, basil stalks tied up with string and basil leaves snipped with scissors.

**4.** Cook, covered, in a 200°C/400°F/Gas Mark 6 oven for approximately 45 minutes or until the juices are thick and shiny. Discard the basil stalks.

**5.** Chop the anchovy fillets and mix with the ragoût. Adjust seasoning but be gentle with the salt as the anchovy fillets are very salty.

This may be served as a side dish or a starter.

## Beignets à l'Orientale

*Oriental-Style Fritters*

| SERVES 6 |
| --- |
| 275 ml/9 fl oz milk |
| 65 g/2½ oz butter |
| 100 g/4 oz strong flour, sieved |
| 3 eggs |
| salt |
| nutmeg |
| cayenne pepper |
| 1 tbsp chopped coriander leaves |
| 1 tsp grated fresh ginger |
| ⅓ peeled avocado, diced |
| 50 g/2 oz grated Parmesan or Feta cheese |
| 50 g/2 oz white crab meat |
| 50 g/2 oz chopped prawns |
| vegetable oil, for frying |

**1.** Make a choux paste by bringing the milk and butter to the boil. Add the sieved flour, beat well until you have a smooth paste and cook for a few minutes on the side of the stove or over a very low heat.

**2.** Spoon the dough-like mixture into a mixing bowl. Cool for about 10 minutes then, using a wooden spoon, add the eggs one by one until smooth.

**3.** Add seasoning and all the other ingredients except the vegetable oil.

**4.** Heat the vegetable oil in a chip pan. Scoop the mixture into small balls with a teaspoon and fry in the hot oil until golden. (When the beignets start to burst, this is the time to remove them from the oil.)

**5.** Place on absorbent paper and serve hot, either plain as they are or with a dip of your own choice.

## 'Spaetzle' de Fromage avec Champignons Sauvages

*Cheese Spätzle with Mushroom Sauce*

| SERVES 6 |
| --- |
| 250 g/9 oz strong flour |
| 4–5 fresh eggs (size 3) |
| salt |
| grated nutmeg |
| 100 g/4 oz grated Gruyère cheese |
| 100 g/4 oz butter |

**1.** Mix the flour, eggs, salt and nutmeg together. Work the mixture very hard in a mixing bowl until bubbles are rising.

**3.** Spread a small part of the dough on a wooden board and shave off thin noodle-like slivers, or spätzle, with a sharp knife. Plunge them into boiling salted water and return to the boil.

**4.** Lift the spätzle out immediately with a skimmer and place them on a large china dish. Sprinkle with part of the grated cheese and keep warm in the oven.

**5.** Repeat procedure until all the dough has been used. Sprinkle the remaining cheese on top.

**6.** Heat the butter until brown and pour over the spätzle. Serve with mushroom sauce and a seasonal salad mixed with a good vinaigrette.

| *Mushroom sauce* |
| --- |
| 50 g/2 oz button mushrooms, sliced |
| 50 g/2 oz mixed dried mushrooms, soaked and chopped |
| 1 shallot, chopped |
| 25 g/1 oz butter |
| 10 ml/½ fl oz dry white wine |
| 120 ml/4 fl oz double cream |
| salt |
| milled black pepper |

**1.** Sweat the shallot in the butter until soft. Add the mushrooms and simmer for a few minutes.

**2.** Deglaze by stirring in the white wine.

**3.** Add the cream, let the mixture boil to a sauce consistency and season to taste.

# 'Strudel' de Légumes aux Deux Coulis

*Vegetable 'Strudel' with Watercress and Red Pepper Sauces*

| SERVES 6 |
| --- |
| 1 medium-sized Savoy cabbage |
| 150 g/5 oz butter |
| 2 artichoke bottoms, cooked |
| 4 carrots, cooked |
| ½ celeriac, cooked and cut into batons 2 cm/¾ in wide |
| 100 g/4 oz button mushrooms, sliced and cooked |
| 100 g/4 oz broccoli fleurettes, cooked |
| 1 tomato, peeled, de-seeded and cut into wedges |
| 100 g/4 oz spinach, cooked and seasoned |
| sea salt |
| pepper |
| caraway seeds |

**1.** Blanch the outer leaves of the cabbage and cool.

**2.** Cut the yellow part into chunks, place in a saucepan with half the butter and a little water. Cover and cook until tender and all the liquid has gone.

**3.** Lay the large cabbage leaves on a cheesecloth and fill as you wish with layers of vegetables, including the yellow cabbage heart. Add the remaining butter in knobs. Season and sprinkle with caraway seeds.

**4.** Wrap the leaves around, and roll into the cheesecloth. Close either end with string. Bind up the middle part with string as well and place into a steamer for about 45 minutes. Meanwhile make the two sauces (see below).

**5.** When ready to serve, remove the strudel from the steamer. Unwrap the cheesecloth and cut with a sharp knife into thick slices. Serve on a large china dish, with the sauces on the side or, for visual effect, poured artistically around the strudel.

| *Watercress Sauce* |
| --- |
| 2 bunches of watercress without stalks |
| 25 ml/1 fl oz water |
| 200 ml/7 fl oz double cream |
| 50 g/2 oz butter |
| salt |
| pepper |

**1.** Place the cress, washed, in a saucepan with the water and cream. Cook, covered, for approximately 12 minutes.

**2.** Put in a liquidizer with the butter and blend until smooth. Season and keep warm.

| *Red Pepper Sauce* |
| --- |
| 2 red peppers, washed, de-seeded and quartered |
| 50 g/2 oz butter |
| ¼ chopped onion |
| 35 ml/1½ fl oz water |
| 25 ml/1 fl oz double cream |

**1.** Heat half the butter in a saucepan. Add the onion and peppers, cover and sweat for a few minutes.

**2.** Add the water and cook slowly, covered, for 10 minutes. Then add the cream and cook for another 15 minutes.

**3.** Pour into a liquidizer. Add the remaining butter and blend until smooth. Season and keep warm.

## Soufflé aux Brocolis avec Tapenade

### Broccoli Soufflé with Almonds and Tapenade

| SERVES 6 |
|---|
| 450 g/1 lb broccoli |
| 600 ml/1 pt milk |
| salt |
| pepper |
| nutmeg |
| 65 g/2½ oz butter |
| 2 eggs |
| 3 egg yolks |
| 75 g/3 oz flour |
| 90 g/3½ oz cheese |
| 50 g/2 oz flaked roasted almonds |
| 6 egg whites |
| 25 g/1 oz flaked plain almonds |

**1.** Boil the broccoli heads, discarding the stalks. Drain and rub through a fine sieve.
**2.** To make the basic soufflé mixture, mix the milk and seasoning and bring three-quarters of the milk and the butter to the boil.
**3.** Mix the whole eggs, yolks and flour with the remaining cold milk and add slowly to the boiling milk.
**4.** Turn the heat down very low. When the mixture thickens, remove from the heat and stir in the cheese.
**5.** Mix the roasted almonds into the mixture and add the broccoli.
**6.** Whip the egg whites until stiff and fold gently into the mixture.
**7.** Pour into a buttered dish sprinkled well with flour or grated cheese. Scatter flaked plain almonds on top.
**8.** Cook for 30–45 minutes at 160°C/325°F/Gas Mark 3.
**9.** Serve with tapenade sauce on the side.

### Sauce Tapenade

A typical sauce from Provence and Corsica.

| |
|---|
| 50 g/2 oz stoned black olives |
| 25 g/1 oz anchovies |
| 1 tsp washed capers |
| 1 tsp strong mustard |
| 120 ml/4 fl oz olive oil |
| pepper |
| juice of ½ lemon |
| salt |

**1.** Pound the olives, anchovies and capers to a paste with a pestle and mortar.
**2.** Add the mustard and gradually the olive oil, until a sauce-like texture is reached.
**3.** Season with some pepper. Add the lemon juice, salt and more pepper to taste.

## Poireaux Braisés Ma Façon

### Young Leeks Braised in a Different Way

| SERVES 6 |
|---|
| 1 kg/2¼ lb young leeks |
| 50 ml/2 fl oz white wine vinegar |
| 10 ml/½ fl oz olive oil |
| 50 g/2 oz icing sugar |
| 100 g/4 oz tomato purée |
| 50 g/2 oz dried currants |
| bouquet garni (thyme, bay leaf and parsley stalks) |

**1.** Cut most of the green from the leeks. Slash lengthwise without cutting through and wash very well.
**2.** Boil for 5 minutes and strain.
**3.** Place in a heavy pan. Add all the other ingredients and cover with water. Simmer for approximately 1 hour. Serve cold.

## Cous-Cous de Légumes

*Vegetarian Cous-Cous*

SERVES 6

| |
|---|
| 250 g/9 oz cous-cous (coarse semolina) |
| 50 ml/2 fl oz olive or sesame oil |
| 2 cloves of garlic, crushed |
| 4 medium-sized carrots, whole |
| 6 small peeled onions, studded with a clove each |
| 2 courgettes, cut into 2.5-cm/1-in pieces |
| 2 heads of fennel, quartered |
| 2 potatoes, peeled and quartered |
| 2 turnips, peeled and quartered |
| 4 ripe tomatoes, quartered |
| 1 red pepper, quartered |
| 1 aubergine, peeled and cut into 2.5-cm/1-in cubes |
| 3 artichoke bottoms, cleaned and quartered |
| 1 leek, washed and cut into 2.5 cm/1-in pieces |
| bunch of flat-leaf parsley, chopped |
| 1 tsp coriander powder |
| 1 tsp cumin powder |
| 1 tsp grated ginger |
| 1 tsp curry powder |
| 2 bay leaves |
| 2 tbsp soy sauce |
| ½ cinnamon stick |
| sea salt |
| pepper |

*Note:* Ideally, a cous-cous steamer should be used for this dish but alternatively you can use a large saucepan with a colander on top which would act like a steamer, or a pressure cooker, which would reduce the length of cooking time.

**1.** Rinse the cous-cous in hot water, then allow it to dry and swell.

**2.** Heat the oil in a large saucepan. Add the garlic and brown slightly, then gradually add all the vegetables, spices, herbs and soy sauce. Cover with water and bring to the boil.

**3.** Place a colander on top, lined with cheese-cloth, and place the cous-cous inside. Cover with an upside-down plate and seal completely with aluminium foil.

**4.** Reduce heat and simmer for about 1½ hours or until the cous-cous is cooked. Some of the vegetables might be overcooked but this brings the best flavour to the vegetable stew. Serve the cous-cous separately.

To garnish, fried soya bean cake (tofu) could be served on the side of the plate.

**Peter Kromberg** *Top, 'Spaetzle' de Fromage avec Champignons Sauvages (page 94) served with a green salad; bottom, Aumônière de Pipérade (page 92)*

**Jane Grigson** *Spinach Roulade with Tomato Sauce (page 105)*

# *Jane Grigson*
## *on*
# *Vegetables*

'It could be said that European civilization – Chinese civilization too – has been founded on the pig. Easily domesticated, omnivorous, housebound, village scavenger, cleaner of scrub and undergrowth, devourer of forest acorns, yet content with a sty – and delightful when cooked or cured, from his snout to his tail.'

With this delightful tribute to the pig, Jane Grigson launched herself as a food writer in 1967, on the publication of *Charcuterie and French Pork Cookery*. Her interest in the subject had been sparked off by her holidays spent in the Touraine region. Although shopping in France became easier with each year that passed there, Jane was acutely aware that she knew very little about charcuterie and that very little had been published about it. She suggested to a friend in the village that he ought to write a book on the subject. She found a publisher for him but somehow ended up writing the manuscript herself – an enormous research project with very few references to help her. The principal sources were Monsieur and Madame Berlu, who ran the boucherie in her own village, Trôo-sur-Loir, and the Cureaus who owned the charcuterie in nearby Montoire. During the four

years it took her to write the book, her family was subjected to an 'unconscionable quantity' of pig. But if Jane's aim in writing it was to reinstate the pig in its variety in English kitchens, it also firmly established her as a cookery writer. The book was even translated into French – which, for an English cookery writer, is a rare privilege.

It was fortuitous that Jane sent a copy of her first manuscript to Elizabeth David because a year later, in 1968, having been approached by *The Observer* with an offer to write for them, Miss David refused but recommended Jane for the job. She has been writing mouth-watering pages ever since. and, along with Elizabeth, has managed to lift the cookery book out of the information and reference section of a library and place it on the shelves of literature.

Jane herself had no cookery training at all and although her mother and grandmother cared a lot about the look, as well as the taste, of food, the diet of the north-east before the war was very boring. 'We got wonderful fish. Full stop.' Vegetables became the mainstay of family meals after Jane's father, a town clerk, forsook meat following his involvement in the closure of a local slaughterhouse, in the 1930s. But when they had the chance, the family could be adventurous in their eating. Jane remembers vividly the first time they ate artichokes. It was in 1955 and her mother found them in a London market. She had 'a vague feeling that eating them was something to do with picking the leaves off', but when Jane reached 'that beautiful cushion of whiskers', she took an enormous mouthful and spent the next two days drinking water.

After reading English at Newnham College, Cambridge, Jane worked as a translator in French and Italian. While she was working for the publishers Rainbird and McLean she met her future husband, Geoffrey Grigson, the poet and critic. Like Jane, he is extremely well read, and between them they have a veritable library of literary memories on which to draw – which is very useful since, for Jane, the subject of food involves history, art, literature, geography, economics and sometimes anthropology.

For one of the first widely read cookery writers, Mrs Beaton, Jane has little time: 'I think she was a very Forsytian person – telling people what they ought to do. This rather gets between you and the food when you read her.' But Jane concedes she had an extraordinary, if not altogether good, influence on the emerging middle classes, especially the class-conscious farming community who were fast buying their town houses. 'Mrs Beaton was there to tell them how to treat their servants, how to organize a dinner, how to lay their table – even how to call on people.' Jane much prefers the writing of Eliza Acton: 'A delightful and elegant cookery writer. You can use her recipes today with pleasure. It's Jane Austen cooking.'

The greatest individual influence on cooking, and according to Jane the greatest chef who ever lived, was Marie-Antoine Carême. 'He raised cooking to a very high, if fussy, art. He regarded pâtisserie as a branch of architecture – and used to create elaborate temples in almond paste.'

But Carême also included in his repertoire of skills such English recipes as hare soup, sea kale, apricot pie and apple pie. Perhaps the fact that he was the first chef to write so many cookery books – eight in all – assured him a wider audience and a greater influence than any chef before him or, in Jane's opinion, since.

Jane still wonders where the French have learned about the quality of food. 'France was a poor country in comparison with England. We've had the money, we've had the food and yet it seems almost as if in England people don't want to know how good food can be.'

Certainly the French take advantage of what is around them. From 1 September no bird is safe, and if families are not hunting they are gathering mushrooms. Jane describes the 'busy silence' of a Sunday hunting cèpes and girolles in the local woods. 'One is isolated, alone, all sense of time goes in the velvet warmth of the young trees. Suddenly some more girolles appear, or the moist brown head of a cèpe – and without meaning to, I shout aloud.'

With the help of their friend Maurice, a vineyard owner and expert on mushroom identification, the Grigsons check their plunder – if there is any doubt they call in the chemist for a second opinion. These types of mushrooms grow in Britain too, but are ignored. A plane leaves Inverness for Paris every week in the mushroom season, loaded with girolles and cèpes. 'The Scots won't eat them.'

In Jane's household, whatever the meal, it is a cause for celebration. There is a feeling of ease in her company, and her generosity shows not only in the hospitality she gives so easily but also in her respect for other writers. She is far from precious about food but does agree with the comment once made by Charles Talleyrand, a great host in his day: 'Can you think of any other pleasure that occurs every day and lasts for an hour?'

**Michael Nadell** *Frutti à la Vanille avec Coulis de Fraises (page 116)*

**Michael Nadell** *Brioches (page 119), Croissants (page 118)*

## *Finocchio alla Parmigiana*

### *Fennel Baked with Parmesan*

SERVES 4

| |
|---|
| 4 heads of fennel, trimmed and quartered |
| pepper |
| 3 tbsp grated Parmesan cheese |

*For the blanc de légumes*

| |
|---|
| 2 tbsp flour |
| 1.2 litres/2 pt water |
| juice of 1 lemon |
| 1 tbsp butter or 2 tbsp oil |

**1.** First prepare the *blanc de légumes:* mix the flour into the water in a bowl. Tip into a pan and add the lemon juice and butter or oil.

**2.** Cook the fennel in the *blanc de légumes* until tender but not floppy, then drain well.

**3.** Arrange the fennel in a buttered gratin dish, garnishing well with pepper. Sprinkle the Parmesan over it and bake in the oven at 200°C/400°F/Gas Mark 6 until the cheese is golden-brown and the juices are bubbling.

## *Chicory Polonaise*

SERVES 4

| |
|---|
| 1 or 2 chicory heads per person |
| *blanc de légumes* mixture (see previous recipe) |
| 15 g/½ oz butter |
| 3 eggs, hard-boiled |
| 2–3 tbsp parsley, chopped |
| 3 tbsp breadcrumbs |

**1.** Blanch the heads of chicory in the *blanc de légumes* until tender, and drain. Toss in half the butter so that the heads are streaked golden-brown.

**2.** Arrange them on a large round dish like wheel spokes. Crumble the hard-boiled eggs, mix with parsley and scatter over the chicory.

**3.** Brown the breadcrumbs in the remaining butter and pour over the top.

## *Creamed Corn Pudding*

SERVES 4

| |
|---|
| 4 fresh corn cobs or 450 g/1 lb tinned corn |
| salt |
| 150 ml/¼ pt whipping cream |
| 150 ml/¼ pt double cream |
| 1 level tsp sugar |
| pepper |
| 50–75 g/2–3 oz butter |

**1.** Cook the corn in boiling salted water until tender, then scrape it off the cob.

**2.** Mix the corn with the cream and sugar and enough salt to bring out the flavour. Add pepper to taste.

**3.** Prepare a gratin dish or individual ramekins by rubbing with about half of the butter. Fill the dishes with the mixture and top with the remaining butter.

**4.** Bake in a 160°C/325°F/Gas Mark 3 oven for 30–45 minutes, or until top is crusted and brown.

This dish can be served as a first course.

# Spinach Roulade with Tomato Sauce

### SERVES 4

| |
|---|
| 175–200 g/6–7 oz cooked spinach, chopped |
| 25 g/1 oz butter |
| 25 g/1 oz flour |
| 150 ml/¼ pt milk |
| 100 g/4 oz onion, finely chopped |
| 175 g/6 oz cottage cheese, drained |
| salt |
| pepper |
| grated nutmeg |
| 4 eggs, separated |
| 1 level tbsp grated Gruyère or Cheddar cheese |
| 1 level tbsp grated Parmesan cheese |

1. To make the filling, melt the butter in a heavy pan and stir in the flour and milk to make a thick sauce. Remove 1 tbsp and set aside.

2. Add the chopped onion to the pan and cook for 3 minutes, then add the cottage cheese and cook for a further 3 minutes. Season well with salt, pepper and nutmeg and set aside.

3. To make the roulade itself, blend the spinach with the reserved spoonful of sauce and the egg yolks. Season and gradually fold in the cheeses.

4. Whisk the egg whites until stiff and fold into the spinach mixture.

5. Spread the mixture over a foil-lined Swiss roll tin 33 × 23 cm/13 × 19 in.

6. Bake at 190°C/375°F/Gas Mark 5 for 15 minutes and then remove from the oven. While it is still warm, put a sheet of greaseproof paper over the roulade and invert it on to the table. Leave to cool for 5 minutes and remove the tin and foil.

7. Reheat the filling and spread it over the roulade, leaving the edges free. Ease it gently into a roll, using the paper to roll it. Holding a hot serving plate close to the roll, give the roulade a flip so that it lands on the dish with its join face-downwards. Serve with the tomato sauce.

| *Tomato Sauce* |
|---|
| 3 large cloves of garlic, chopped |
| 1 large onion, chopped |
| 100 g/4 oz streaky bacon, chopped |
| 2 tbsp butter or bacon fat |
| 1 large carrot, diced |
| 900 g/2 lb tomatoes, skinned and chopped (or 800-g/1-lb 12-oz tin) |
| 150 ml/¼ pt dry white or red wine |
| salt |
| pepper |
| sugar |
| dried oregano |
| chopped fresh basil |

1. Cook the garlic, onion and bacon gently in the fat.

2. Add the carrot, tomatoes and wine, breaking the mixture down with a wooden spoon. Raise the heat and cook very fast, uncovered, for 15 minutes (more slowly if you are using tinned tomatoes).

3. After 10 minutes, add the seasonings and oregano. Add the basil just before serving.

**Michael Nadell** *Top left, Truffe au Chocolat (page 114); top right, Fruits au Caramel (page 117); bottom left, Tuiles aux Amandes (page 118); bottom right, Tarte aux Pommes (page 114)*

# Carottes à la Forestière

*Forester's Carrots*

| SERVES 4 |
| --- |
| 675 g/1½ lb carrots, sliced |
| 150 ml/¼ pt beef stock |
| nutmeg |
| 225 g/8 oz mushrooms, sliced |
| a little butter |
| 150 ml/¼ pt double cream |
| 1 tbsp parsley, chopped |
| 1 tbsp chives, chopped |
| salt |
| pepper |
| lemon juice |
| 4 bread baps |

**1.** Cook the carrots in the beef stock with a little nutmeg until the liquid is reduced to a syrupy consistency.

**2.** Fry the mushrooms in butter until they are lightly browned.

**3.** Add the mushrooms, cream and herbs to the cooked carrots. Stir gently until the sauce is thick enough to coat the vegetables. Season to taste with salt, pepper and lemon juice.

**4.** Set the oven to 200°C/400°F/Gas Mark 6. Split the baps into two and hollow out. Brush with melted butter and put into the oven for 10–15 minutes to crisp up.

**5.** Pile the mushroom and carrot mixture into the bases of the baps. Replace their lids and serve immediately.

# Artichokes Stuffed with Purée of Broad Beans

| SERVES 4 |
| --- |
| 4 globe artichokes |
| 1.4 kg/3 lb broad beans |
| 2 tbsp vinegar |
| salt |
| 900 ml/1½ pt water |
| large lump of butter |
| 3–4 tbsp cream |
| lemon juice |
| savory, chopped |

**1.** Soak the artichokes upside down in salted water to remove any insects from the leaves.

**2.** Add the vinegar and salt to a large pan of water and bring to the boil.

**3.** Cut the stalks from the artichokes and place them head-down in the boiling water for 30 minutes. Test them by taking a leaf from the base – if it is tender, they are ready.

**4.** Drain the artichokes upside down in a colander. When they are cool enough to handle, pull out the centre leaves to expose the choke. Scrape the choke away with a teaspoon.

**5.** Shell, cook and skin the broad beans.

**6.** Sieve the beans into a clean pan and reheat with the butter, cream and a squeeze or two of lemon juice.

**7.** Mix in the chopped savory and fill the centre of each artichoke with the purée.

To eat, remove the outer leaves and dip them into the centre mixture. Eat the bottom with a knife and fork.

## Peas in the French Style

SERVES 4

| 1 small lettuce (or 8 outer leaves of a large lettuce), shredded |
| 6 spring onions, chopped |
| 450 g/1 lb shelled peas |
| 2 young carrots, chopped |
| 2 tsp sugar |
| 1 tbsp chopped parsley |
| ¼ tsp salt |
| 3 tbsp butter |
| 4 tbsp water |

**1.** Make a bed of lettuce in the bottom of a pan.
**2.** Place the onions, peas, carrots, sugar, parsley, butter and ¼ tsp salt on top. Add the water.
**3.** Cover the pan tightly and stew for 20 minutes.
**4.** Taste and add more salt if required.

## Potatoes with Mushroom Sauce in the Russian Style

SERVES 4

| 675–900 g/1½–2 lb potatoes |
| 1 onion, chopped |
| 350 g/12 oz mushrooms, chopped |
| 40 g/1½ oz butter |
| 1 heaped tsp flour |
| 300 ml/½ pt soured cream |
| 1 tsp dill or fennel, chopped |
| salt |
| pepper |

**1.** Scrub and boil the potatoes, without peeling them.
**2.** Cook the onion and mushrooms in the butter for 15 minutes.

**3.** Stir in the flour thoroughly and then add the soured cream slowly and heat carefully. It must not boil.
**4.** Add most of the dill or fennel, and season with salt and pepper, leaving a little of the herb aside for garnishing later.
**5.** When the potatoes are cooked, remove their skins and slice them into a hot serving dish.
**6.** Spread the mushroom sauce evenly over the top of the potatoes and garnish with the remaining dill or fennel.

## Kartoffelpuffer

*Potato Pancakes*

SERVES 4–6

| 675 g/1½ lb peeled potatoes |
| 90 g/3½ oz grated onion |
| 2 eggs |
| 175 g/6 oz plain flour |
| pinch of salt |
| lard |
| 1 eating apple (sliced, cooked in a little butter and tossed in sugar) or 50 g/2 oz apple purée |

**1.** Using the coarse side of a grater, shred the potatoes into a bowl.
**2.** Mix in the onion, then the eggs, flour and salt, and stir thoroughly.
**3.** In a heavy frying pan heat enough lard to make 5 mm/¼ in depth of fat. When it is hot, place 4 tbsp of the mixture in a heap in the pan and flatten it with the back of a spoon to make a pancake 12 cm/5 in across. Turn the pancake when the edges are golden-brown and crisp, and cook the other side.
**4.** Drain well and garnish with apple slices or purée.

**John Huber** *Champagne Sorbet (page 123)*

**John Huber** *Gâteau Forêt Noir (page 124)*

# *Michael Nadell*
## ——*on*——
# *Desserts*

Six o'clock in the morning is not an unusual time to sit down to a meal in the Nadell household – in fact it has become the norm since Stella and Michael Nadell expanded their pâtisserie business in Islington a year ago. The idea of eating at such an odd hour might make your digestive juices quail, but Michael and Stella have adjusted pluckily to consuming three courses and a bottle of wine while the sun rises.

'We don't eat to live in our house – we live to eat,' says Michael, a little guiltily, knowing he's breaking every rule there is about healthy eating. But eating is one of the few pleasures he and Stella can allow themselves while the pâtisserie continues to expand. And business is booming. Michael has to make 450 lb of shortcrust pastry, 700 lb of puff and 1400 lb of sweet pastry to meet one week's production; 9000 eggs are beaten into 2000 lb of flour, 800 lb of butter and 660 lb of sugar – not to mention the 130 gallons of cream or the 100 gallons of milk or the 220 lb of chocolate that are used.

Around ten o'clock at night the smell down White Lion Street as you approach the pâtisserie is incredible – a mixture of the thousand croissants that are baked every night, the Danish pastries with their apricot glaze, the Truffe au Chocolat, Passion-Fruit Charlotte – indeed the full aromatic force of the 81 items on the Nadell menu.

The House of Commons is a regular customer, ensuring some ever-widening girths among the Honourable Gentlemen, and Dickins and Jones in Regent Street take the croissants, Danish pastries and gateaux – but further than that I cannot divulge because Michael supplies those hotels in London that cannot afford their own pâtisserie section but would like to convince their customers otherwise. Michael is quite flattered by the deception – after all it is a compliment to him that they wish to identify with his products.

The Nadells' business has developed in response to an enormous gap in quality pâtisserie in England. Comparisons between our bread and cake shops and those in France are embarrassing – so few pâtisseries here produce good things. But Michael simply will not compromise over ingredients – and always makes the product first and then costs it out, rather than setting the price first and having to cut corners to keep within the margins. His fruit bill alone is over £2000 a week to ensure that his fresh fruit tarts are perfect. He uses 24 bottles each of kirsch, sherry and rum, and 48 bottles of grand marnier – more than 140 bottles of liqueur a week. Encouragingly, the demand for these high-quality products continues to grow, and the Nadell pâtisserie is literally snapped up as soon as it is out of the oven.

Michael had a very sound, British training at Westminster College – the first cookery school in England. After graduating in 1965 he worked in the pâtisserie sections of six hotels and in his last job was master pâtissier with a staff of ten under him. But in the hierarchy of hotel kitchens Michael had gone as far as he could go, and he was left with two options – either to teach or to work for himself. He chose the latter and started his own business in Hackney in 1982.

Although he has never been tempted to work outside England, some of Michael's inspiration does come from gazing into the windows of French pâtisseries. After seeing a chocolate mousse with orange and crème anglais, he came back and tried it out. He now sells more than 200 'Indulgents' a week.

His recipe for croissants is the result of weeks of experimentation. The greatest problem with them is how quickly they become tired and stale. He knew that the more butter he added, the longer the shelf-life but the greater the danger of a fatty residue on the roof of the mouth. So he experimented with all possible combinations to arrive at the Nadell croissant. Even now he tastes one of the batch every evening, to ensure that his recipe has been followed to the letter.

Michael possesses all the attributes required of a master pâtissier – patience, meticulous accuracy and the ability to function on only a few hours' sleep. He often uses the early hours of the morning to do his sugarwork, which is 'the greatest test in pastrywork because it demands more skills than anything else I do'. He has to his credit seven gold and two silver awards for his sugar pieces and is undoubtedly one of England's leading craftsmen in the special skill of sugarwork. His creations are not restricted to flowers, or fruit or vegetables – although he does these beautifully – but extend to pieces such as Liberace's piano, which was commissioned by his fan club, and a bird of paradise for a competition, which necessitated Michael spending hours in the Victoria and Albert Museum checking the plumage.

This kind of commitment and dedication to both a business and a profession are hard to match. Inevitably in this kind of work, with its odd and long hours, the staff turnover is quick, and this makes Michael's job doubly difficult: he has to be there all the time to ensure that the standards of the products bearing the Nadell name are as high as he wants. There are no days off for the trout fishing which he loves.

One day Michael would like to relax a little and perhaps extend his cooking skills to include meat and fish dishes – perhaps in a wine bar with a small but interesting menu. Whatever he chooses, it would have to be connected with food.

He is convinced that 'you have to love eating to cook well', and he regards every meal he cooks for Stella, even if it is at six o'clock in the morning, as equivalent to giving her a present. 'Cooking a meal is my way of giving pleasure.' And, although he turns out the most exquisite desserts, for Michael the perfect way to end a meal is quite simple: 'a piece of cheese and a glass of port'.

# Tarte aux Poires Bourdaloue

*Bourdaloue Pear Flan*

SERVES APPROX 10

| |
|---|
| 10 pear halves, well drained |
| 600 ml/1 pt crème pâtissière (see recipe p 119) |
| three-quarters-cooked pâte sucrée flan case (24 cm/9½ in diameter) (see recipe p 120) |
| 1 tbsp eau de vie Poire William |
| 50 g/2 oz flaked almonds |

**1.** Pour a thin layer (200 ml/7 fl oz) of hot crème pâtissière into the flan base.
**2.** Place the well-drained pears on the crème pâtissière in the flan and sprinkle them with eau de vie Poire William.
**3.** Cover with the remaining crème pâtissière and sprinkle flaked almonds on the top.
**4.** Place in the oven at 200°C/400°F/Gas Mark 6 for 10–15 minutes until coloured.
**5.** Remove from the oven and cool. Remove the ring and dust with icing sugar, then place under the grill to glaze the top.

# Tarte aux Pommes

*Apple Flan*

SERVES 10

| |
|---|
| raw pâte sucrée flan case (25 cm/10 in diameter × 3 cm/1¼ in high) (see recipe p 120) |
| 300 ml/½ pt crème pâtissière (see recipe p 119) |
| 1.4 kg/3 lb Bramley apples, cored and peeled |
| 50 g/2 oz sugar |
| 100 g/4 oz apricot glaze (see recipe p 120) |

**1.** Place the flan on a baking tray – having pricked the base with a fork.
**2.** Spread the crème pâtissière into the flan case, making a dome in the middle.
**3.** Cut the apples in half and cut into 3-mm/⅛-in slices.
**4.** Arrange the slices of apple in concentric circles forming a pyramid as you work from the outer edge to the middle. Sprinkle sugar between the layers (this helps the apples to cook).
**5.** Sprinkle sugar over the finished pyramid (which should be quite high as the apples will sink during cooking).
**6.** Place in a 200°C/400°F/Gas Mark 6 oven for 35–40 minutes – until the flan is nicely coloured and the apples are soft (to test for this insert a knife into the centre of the flan as you would with a fruit cake). Cool.
**8.** Brush with apricot glaze.

# Truffe au Chocolat

*Chocolate Truffle*

SERVES APPROX 10

| |
|---|
| 1 sheet of chocolate sponge (see recipe p 120) |
| 50 ml/2 fl oz rum |
| 50 ml/2 fl oz stock syrup (see recipe p 120) |
| 600 ml/1 pt whipping cream |
| 425 g/15 oz plain chocolate |
| 25 g/1 oz cocoa powder |

**1.** Using a stainless steel ring (23 cm/9 in diameter × 4.5 cm/1¾ in high) cut out a circular sponge base from the sponge sheet.
**2.** Put the stainless steel ring on a cake board and place the sponge base inside the ring. Brush with a mixture of the rum and stock syrup.
**3.** Lightly whip the cream. Melt the chocolate (to a temperature of 60°C/125°F), pour it into

the cream and fold together with a metal whisk.
**4.** Fill the ring to the top with this mousse mixture. Set in the fridge to cool.
**5.** Dust with cocoa powder, remove the ring (this can be made easier by warming the ring with a hot cloth) and serve.

# Bagatelle aux Fraises et Bananes

### Strawberry and Banana Bagatelle

SERVES APPROX 10

| |
|---|
| **1 genoise sponge (see recipe p 120)** |
| **50 ml/2 fl oz grand marnier** |
| **50 ml/2 fl oz stock syrup (see recipe p 120)** |
| **50 g/2 oz raspberry jam** |
| **300 ml/½ pt crème Chantilly (see recipe p 119)** |
| **100 g/4 oz fresh strawberries** |
| **1 banana, sliced lengthways** |
| **icing sugar for dusting** |
| **50 g/2 oz green marzipan** |
| **50 g/2 oz hazelnuts, ground** |

**1.** Split the sponge into 3 tiers.
**2.** Add the grand marnier to the stock syrup and brush the bottom layer with the mixture.
**3.** Spread the bottom of the second layer of sponge with raspberry jam and then place it on the first layer. Brush with grand marnier syrup.
**4.** Spread half the crème Chantilly mixture over the second layer of sponge using a palette knife. Place a ring of strawberries round the edge of the sponge, and fill the centre with sliced banana. Dust surface with icing sugar and cover with a little more crème Chantilly.
**5.** Place the third tier of sponge on the top and press flat. Brush with grand marnier syrup. Spread the top and sides with crème Chantilly (leave a little over for the garnish later) and

cover the sides of the sponge with hazelnut crumbs. Place a disc of green marzipan on top of the sponge and decorate with rosettes of crème Chantilly and half-strawberries.

# Buche au Coco Lopez

### Lopez Coconut Log

SERVES APPROX 10

| |
|---|
| **1 sheet of vanilla sponge (see recipe p 120)** |
| **150 ml/¼ pt stock syrup (see recipe p 120)** |
| **150 ml/¼ pt coconut liqueur** |
| **50 g/2 oz apricot jam, for glaze** |
| **100 g/4 oz desiccated coconut (which has been roasted)** |

*For the coconut cream*

| |
|---|
| **450 ml/¾ pt crème pâtissière (see recipe p 119)** |
| **150 ml/¼ pt coconut liqueur** |
| **225 g/8 oz cream of coconut** |
| **5 leaves of gelatine (18 g/¾ oz)** |
| **300 ml/½ pt whipping cream** |

**1.** To make the coconut cream, beat together the cold crème pâtissière, coconut liqueur and cream of coconut. Then beat in the warm melted gelatine and fold in the stiffly beaten cream.
**2.** Line a gutter mould with a piece of the vanilla sponge. Brush with a mixture of the stock syrup and coconut liqueur, and then spread with coconut cream.
**3.** Place another piece of sponge on top and brush it with the liqueur syrup. Fill the mould with the remainder of the coconut cream.
**4.** On top place a strip of sponge which will form the base when the mould is turned over. Brush with syrup.
**5.** Chill well. When chilled, turn out of the mould, brush with apricot glaze and immediately sprinkle all over with toasted coconut.

## Frutti à la Vanille avec Coulis de Fraises

**Vanilla Frutti with Strawberry Coulis**

| SERVES APPROX 10 |
|---|
| 1 sheet of vanilla sponge (see recipe p 120) |
| 225 g/8 oz raspberry jam |
| 450 g/1 lb assorted fresh fruits in season |
| 200 ml/7 fl oz stock syrup (see recipe p 120) |
| ½ vanilla pod, split |
| 15 g/½ oz gelatine |
| 450 ml/¾ pt whipping cream |
| 150 g/5 oz apricot glaze (see recipe p 120) |

**1.** Sandwich four rectangular strips of sponge with raspberry jam and press well together. (Leave enough sponge to form the flan base.)
**2.** Slice the sponge into strips 5 mm/¼ in thick. Place a stainless steel ring (23 cm/9 in diameter × 4.5 cm/1¾ in high) on silicone paper and line with vertical strips of sponge.
**3.** Inside the steel ring place a layer of fresh fruit slices.
**4.** To make the mousse, bring the syrup and split vanilla pod to the boil. Add the soaked gelatine.
**5.** Pass the hot syrup through a sieve, and cool. As the mixture begins to set, fold in the whipped cream.
**6.** Spread a layer of mousse on top of the fresh fruits in the ring and continue spreading alternate layers of fresh fruit and mousse – ending with a layer of mousse.
**7.** Place a circle of sponge (taken from the sponge sheet) on top of the flan. Chill well in the fridge.
**8.** When the flan is chilled, turn it over and remove the ring. Brush the top and sides with apricot glaze. Serve with the coulis de fraises.

| Coulis de Fraises |
|---|
| 100 g/4 oz fresh strawberries |
| 2 tbsp stock syrup (see recipe p 120) |
| 1 tbsp grand marnier |

Liquidize all the ingredients and pass through a sieve.

## Charlotte aux Abricots

**Apricot Charlotte**

| SERVES APPROX 10 |
|---|
| 20 biscuits à la cuillère (sponge fingers) |
| 1 sponge circle from a Victoria or genoise sponge (see recipe p 120) |
| 150 ml/¼ pt milk |
| 100 g/4 oz caster sugar |
| 35 g/1¼ oz gelatine (10 leaves) |
| 600 ml/1 pt apricot pulp (tinned apricots with a little juice, pulped in a blender) |
| 600 ml/1 pt whipping cream |
| 20 apricot halves |
| 100 g/4 oz apricot glaze (see recipe p 120) |

**1.** Line the sides of a stainless steel ring or cake tin (23 cm/9 in diameter × 4.5 cm/1¾ in high) with the biscuits à la cuillère. Trim them to the top of the ring.
**2.** Place a thin slice of sponge on the bottom of the ring.
**3.** Boil the milk and sugar, add the soaked gelatine and then the apricot pulp.
**4.** Pass this mixture through a sieve and cool it until it begins to set.
**5.** Whip the cream lightly and fold it into the setting mixture. Fill the prepared mould almost to the top and set in the fridge.
**6.** Place the well-drained apricot halves on the top of the charlotte and glaze with the apricot glaze.

# Paris Brest

SERVES APPROX 10

| |
|---|
| 300 ml/½ pt water |
| 100 g/4 oz butter |
| pinch of sugar |
| pinch of salt |
| 150 g/5 oz plain flour |
| 4–5 eggs (depending on size) |
| 1–2 beaten eggs for egg wash |
| 25 g/1 oz flaked almonds |

*For the filling*

| |
|---|
| 50 g/2 oz crushed praline |
| 300 ml/½ pt crème pâtissière (see recipe p 119) |
| 300 ml/½ pt whipping cream |
| icing sugar for dusting top of dessert |

**1.** Bring the water, butter, sugar and salt to the boil in a pan.

**2.** Lower the heat and beat in the flour until the mixture leaves the sides of the pan.

**3.** Beat in the eggs one at a time until the mixture drops easily from a spoon.

**4.** Pipe the mixture in a thick circle on to a greased baking tray – the outside of the circle should be 25 cm/10 in in diameter.

**5.** Brush with beaten egg and cover liberally with flaked almonds.

**6.** Cook in the oven at 190°C/375°F/Gas Mark 5 until well risen, golden and crisp.

**7.** Remove from the oven and immediately slice in half to form two rings.

**8.** Beat the crushed praline into the crème pâtissière and then fold in the whipped cream.

**9.** Pipe this filling on to the bottom half of the Paris Brest – using all the filling.

**10.** Place the upper half on top of the filling and dust the Paris Brest with icing sugar.

# Fruits au Caramel

*Caramelized Fruits*

| |
|---|
| 1 bunch of grapes or 1 orange |
| 150 ml/¼ pt water |
| 450 g/1 lb granulated sugar |
| 1 tsp liquid glucose |
| ¼ tsp lemon juice |

*Note:* Sugar is preferably boiled in a copper sugar boiler as it transfers heat better. Failing this, a stainless steel pan will do. Whichever is used, the pan must be absolutely clean.

**1.** The day before the fruit is required, wash the grapes in hot water and separate them so that there are 2 grapes on each stalk. Or peel the orange, removing all pith, then break it into segments. Place the fruit on kitchen paper in a warm place overnight to dry.

**2.** Next day, bring the water, sugar and glucose to the boil and skim off any froth. While the sugar boils, wash down the inside of the pan with cold water. This will stop crystals forming.

**3.** When the sugar reaches the hard-ball stage (150°C/260°F) it will only be necessary to wash the sides occasionally.

**4.** When the sugar reaches the hard-crack stage (160°C/320°F) add the lemon juice and place the pan in cold water for a few minutes to stop the sugar cooking any further. The addition of lemon juice will help to stop crystallization. If the sugar cools and is too thick, reheat gently.

**5.** Dip the grapes into the hard-crack sugar and allow the excess to drain off before setting on a well-oiled baking tray. Dip in half of each orange segment and set on the baking tray for 1 minute before dipping the other half.

## Tuiles aux Amandes

### Almond Tuiles

| |
|---|
| 225 g/8 oz nibbed almonds |
| 225 g/8 oz caster sugar |
| 25 g/1 oz plain flour |
| 6 egg whites |
| a little clarified butter |

**1.** Mix together the almonds, sugar and flour and then beat in the egg whites and leave the mixture to rest for ½ day.
**2.** Brush a baking tray with clarified butter.
**3.** Place 1 tsp tuile mixture on the tray and press flat with a fork which has been dipped in water. Repeat. Leave plenty of space between the tuiles.
**4.** Bake at 200°C/400°F/Gas Mark 6 until dark round the edges and pale gold in the centre.
**5.** Keeping the tray at the mouth of the oven, remove the tuiles with a palette knife and place over a rolling pin to set. (N.B. It is important to work quickly or the mixture will set. If it does, then simply reheat in the oven.)

The tuiles are far nicer if eaten within a few hours of being made – but they can be stored in an airtight tin.

## Croissants

| MAKES 10 CROISSANTS |
|---|
| 15 g/½ oz yeast |
| 25 g/1 oz sugar |
| 150 ml/¼ pt water |
| 150 ml/¼ pt milk |
| 300 g/10 oz butter |
| pinch of salt |
| 450 g/1 lb strong plain flour |
| 1–2 beaten eggs for egg wash |

**1.** Dissolve the yeast and sugar in a mixture of the water and milk.
**2.** Mix 50 g/2 oz of the butter, salt and flour.
**3.** Add the yeast mixture to the butter and flour mixture and beat well until smooth. Place in a plastic bag in the fridge for 2 hours.
**4.** Beat the remaining butter into a thin layer.
**5.** Roll out the dough into a rectangle. Place the butter on one half of the rectangle and fold the other half over it.
**6.** Roll out into another rectangle. Fold the right-hand third over the centre third (1) and then fold the left-hand section over the top (2).
**7.** Rest the pastry for ½ hour in the fridge.
**8.** With a folded edge towards you, roll out the pastry again and fold it in thirds as before.
**9.** Leave it in the fridge until next day.
**10.** With a folded edge towards you again, repeat the process a third time.
**11.** Next roll out the pastry 5 mm/¼ in thick and 35 cm/14 in wide, and as long as possible. Cut it in half lengthways and then into elongated triangles (3).
**12.** From the base of the triangle roll each croissant to the tip. Place the rolls of pastry in a greased baking tray with the tip of the triangle underneath and then form them into the crescent shape (this will stop the croissant coming undone). Brush with beaten egg.
**13.** Put in a warm place for the dough to prove for 40 minutes–1 hour. The croissants should become twice their size.
**14.** Brush again with beaten egg – carefully because they could collapse at this stage.
**15.** Cook in the oven at 220°C/425°F/Gas Mark 7 for 15–20 minutes – until golden and the bottom is browned also.

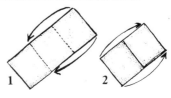

# Brioches

MAKES 12 INDIVIDUAL BRIOCHES OR 2 LARGE ONES

| |
|---|
| 15 g/½ oz yeast |
| 50 g/2 oz sugar |
| 65 ml/2½ fl oz water |
| 4 eggs |
| 450 g/1 lb strong plain flour |
| large pinch of salt |
| 225 g/8 oz butter |
| 1–2 beaten eggs for egg wash |

**For basic dough**

**1.** Dissolve together the yeast and sugar in the water. Beat in the eggs.
**2.** Add the flour and salt and beat to a stiff dough.
**3.** When the mixture is smooth, beat in the butter in small pieces. (The finished paste should have a silky appearance.)
**4.** Place the dough in a polythene bag and rest it overnight in the fridge.

**For brioche à tête**

**5.** Weigh the dough into 50-g/2-oz pieces and roll it into balls.
**6.** With the back of your hand make a deep indent into each ball of dough.

**7.** Place the dough (heavy end first) into a fluted brioche mould. Push the 'little hat' towards the centre, leaving it just protruding above the body of the dough. Egg-wash the top of the brioche.
**8.** Allow it to prove in a warm place until it is double the size. Egg-wash again.
**9.** Cook the dough at 220°C/425°F/Gas Mark 7 for 20 minutes.

# Crème Pâtissière

| |
|---|
| 600 ml/1 pt milk |
| ½ split vanilla pod |
| 100 g/4 oz caster sugar |
| 50 g/2 oz flour |
| 10 g/¼ oz custard powder |
| 2 eggs |

**1.** Bring the milk and vanilla pod slowly to the boil.
**2.** Cream together the sugar, flour, custard powder and eggs.
**3.** Add half the boiled milk and whisk until smooth.
**4.** Return the mixture to the pan and bring to the boil, whisking all the time to avoid lumps forming.
**5.** Pour into a bowl and put buttered paper on top of the mixture to prevent a skin forming.
**6.** Cool the mixture by placing a rack under the bowl (it is important to let air circulate or else the mixture could turn sour).

# Crème Chantilly

| |
|---|
| 300 ml/½ pt whipping cream |
| 25 g/1 oz caster sugar |
| drop of vanilla essence |

Simply whip these ingredients together to make a sweetened cream.

## Stock Syrup

| |
|---|
| **600 ml/1 pt water** |
| **450 g/1 lb sugar** |

Boil the water and sugar together, then pass the liquid through muslin. Store in a cool place.

This syrup is used to moisten the sponge in gateaux, for mousse mixtures and for poaching fruit. For liqueur-flavoured syrup use half syrup and half liqueur.

## Apricot Glaze

| |
|---|
| **450 g/1 lb apricot jam** |
| **100 g/4 oz granulated sugar** |
| **150 ml/¼ pt apricot syrup from tin of apricots** |
| **150 ml/¼ pt apricot pulp (tinned apricots which have been liquidized)** |

Bring all the ingredients very gently to the boil and then pass through a fine sieve.

## Pâte Sucrée

| |
|---|
| ENOUGH TO LINE 2 × 24-CM 9½-IN FLAN TINS |
| **350 g/12 oz butter** |
| **175 g/6 oz sugar** |
| **few drops of vanilla essence** |
| **2 eggs** |
| **450 g/1 lb self-raising flour** |

**1.** Cream together the butter, sugar and vanilla essence.
**2.** Beat in the eggs.
**3.** Fold in the flour.

Always work this paste on a cold surface, dusting your work surface with the minimum of flour. Work the paste into a smooth ball – taking care not to overwork it.

## Genoise Sponge

| |
|---|
| **100 g/4 oz caster sugar** |
| **4 eggs** |
| **100 g/4 oz self-raising flour** |
| **50 g/2 oz butter, melted** |

**1.** Whisk together the sugar and eggs in a bowl over hot water until the mixture forms ribbons.
**2.** Fold in the flour.
**3.** Fold in the melted butter.
**4.** Pour the mixture into a lined, round sponge tin and bake at 190°C/375°F/Gas Mark 5 for about 30 minutes. It should be well risen and spongy to touch.

## Vanilla Sponge

| |
|---|
| **100 g/4 oz caster sugar** |
| **4 eggs** |
| **100 g/4 oz self-raising flour** |

**1.** Whisk together the sugar and eggs in a bowl over hot water until the mixture forms ribbons.
**2.** Fold in the flour.
**3.** Pour the mixture into a baking tray lined with silicone paper and spread thinly.
**4.** Bake in the oven at 230°C/450°F/Gas Mark 8 for about 5 minutes. Cool.

**For chocolate sponge** use 50 g/2 oz cornflour and 50 g/2 oz cocoa powder, mixed together, instead of the flour.

# *John Huber*
## —on—
# *Desserts*

'Pastry-cooks in this country are definitely second-class citizens,' says John Huber, and it's very rare they ever find an opportunity to practise their craft without compromises. Whereas in Switzerland the highest standard of pastry-work can be found even in local pâtisseries, in England the few opportunities for such high-quality creative work are in large hotels. But even then the master pâtissier has always been second in the kitchen hierarchy to the chef de cuisine. The only other option is to try industry but then, likely as not, the job will be as production manager for mass-produced chocolate éclairs. Certainly quality and any personal touch must give way to the demands of efficient machines. John has had experience of this, for he spent two years working like that for a large bakery company and he remembers the sheer frustration of eighteen months of 'tailoring' a mille-feuille slice to both the measurements of the machine and an economical price tag; considerations which were not just irrelevant in Switzerland, they were taboo.

John believes the meticulous attention to the detail in a pâtissier's training may have something to do with the fact that many of the famous chefs, like Carême and Nignon, were trained as

pastry-cooks. 'But even with perfectly measured ingredients a recipe can work a dozen times and then the next time it goes wrong.' Even the atmosphere in which flour is stored can alter its water content, and normally firm dough will become runny.

John Huber was sixteen when he began his training, in 1948. Eric Meng, the confiseur, was a hard taskmaster, but it was from Meng that John learned most of his skills. 'All I ever did was to copy my boss – but it never looked as good as his.' Lemon cakes were always labelled with characteristic 'citron' lettering – a Meng tradition which John in turn passed on to junior apprentices elsewhere after he had qualified.

John's first job was at Halsingbord, Sweden, for the suppliers to King Gustav. Every Sunday their job was to supply the desserts, usually ice creams, set in spun sugar and kept cold in elaborate ice sculptures – perhaps in the wings of a swan or the petals of a water lily. Sculpting a block of ice using chisels and hammers is a far cry from the intricacies of pastry-work, but it takes courage both to work and to watch.

Before he began lecturing in 1967, John spent roughly eight years working as a qualified pâtissier in Sweden, Switzerland and Italy – and the following eight years in this country as an employee of J. Lyons. The only real consolation he found working in industry was the regular hours – not an unimportant consideration when there is a wife and son to consider.

While he was working for Lyons, John came across a number of youngsters in the kitchens who 'given the right type of training would have been excellent pastry-cooks, but there was nowhere for them to get a specialized training'. They could now, as John runs an advanced pastry course at Slough Catering College, as well as full-time, part-time and day-release courses for beginners and apprentices. 'They come out of school at sixteen, green – they've never seen a kitchen, they don't know what a machine is, they've never handled a knife. They look at a chef's knife and nearly faint.' Students usually begin their courses learning the principles of pastry-making: 'nothing can substitute for butter', and all ingredients should be at room temperature. For sweet shortcrust remember to cream the fat, sugar and egg first before you mix them into the flour.

Accuracy in the measurement of ingredients and understanding the effect they have on each other are crucial to a good result. Through question and answer during John's working demonstration of mousses, students learn that every fresh fruit can be used to make a mousse except pineapple and kiwi. Their special enzymes, recently famed for their ability to break down body fat, also, it seems, break down the structure of gelatine. So the two fruits have to be cooked first to avert disaster. As crucial as flavouring to the success of a mousse or soufflé is a stiff meringue, and once again, John has advice for his students: clean bowls (stainless steel or copper are best), clean whisks and eggs at room temperature are essential. 'And whatever anybody else says, use a machine because it can beat the mixture quickly and firmly.' Al-

ways add a pinch of salt to the egg whites to break up the albumen and when the whites look foamy begin to add sugar: 50 g/2 oz to 1 egg white. By the time the mixture has peaked, half the sugar should have been added. 'But instead of switching off the machine, beat the living daylights out of the mixture. Then turn off and add the rest of the sugar either with a spatula or using speed No. 1 on the mixer.'

As in all further education courses, budgets have to be tight at Slough. Foie gras and truffles have to give way to cheaper ingredients. Peanuts are substituted for almonds and essence added; crystallized apples dyed green and red are used instead of cherries and angelica. But this constant need for economy John finds more of a challenge than a compromise and the food in the training restaurant is very good indeed.

John may have opted to teach in a technical college but he has not lost touch with his fellow cooks both in industry and hotels. Indeed, his connections were strengthened in 1976 when he became a member of Club Nine. Through the club his students can gain valuable experience and good contacts when they leave college.

John's greatest skill is working with chocolate. 'It's a raw material that requires a lot of skill but it does give you scope to express yourself. And when you get that sheen which lasts for months you know you've dominated the raw material.' John continues to experiment with chocolate and often spends weekends in his shed at home surrounded by lines of chocolate 'glue pots' and trays of white icing sugar.

From the elaborate *pièces montées* of Carême, sweet dishes have been simplified more and more, and according to John, 'so long as everyone is watching the calories the trend towards light simple dishes will continue.' But he is convinced that in fifteen years or so, tastes will have come full circle and rich, old-fashioned desserts will once again grace our dinner tables.

## William Pear Sorbet

SERVES 12

| |
|---|
| 500 ml/1 pt purée of pears (fresh or tinned) |
| 600 ml/1 pt water |
| 1 kg/2.2 lb sugar |
| 1 tbsp lemon juice |
| 2 tbsp Poire William liqueur |

**1.** Set the freezer compartment of the fridge to the coldest setting.
**2.** Peel, core and halve the pears.
**3.** Poach them in a stock syrup: bring the water to the boil, stir in the sugar until well dissolved, return to the boil and simmer for 1 minute.
**4.** Cut up the pears and liquidize with the stock syrup. Add the lemon juice and liqueur.
**5.** Tip into a shallow dish and place in the freezer compartment until firm.

## Champagne Sorbet

SERVES 12

| |
|---|
| 800 ml/1⅜ pt stock syrup (see previous recipe) |
| 450 ml/¾ pt champagne |
| 40 g/1½ oz sugar |
| juice of 2 lemons |
| 2 egg whites |

**1.** Mix the syrup and the champagne well. Chill in the freezer at the coldest setting.
**2.** Dissolve the remaining sugar in a little hot water, add the lemon juice and leave to cool. Whip the egg whites until stiff, and beat in the cold sugar solution.
**3.** When the champagne mixture is half-frozen, fold in the egg white and sugar mixture. Mix well and re-freeze until set. (This takes about 4 hours.)

## Parfait Au Praline

SERVES 12

| |
|---|
| 50 g/2 oz sugar |
| 25 g/1 oz nibbed almonds, roasted |
| 5 egg yolks |
| 185 g/6½ oz icing sugar |
| ½ tsp vanilla essence |
| 5 egg whites |
| 150 g/¼ pt whipping cream |
| *sauce au kirsch* **made from 300 ml/½ pt whipped cream, few drops of vanilla essence, and sugar and kirsch to taste** |

**1.** To make the praline, melt the sugar to a dark caramel, then add the hot nibbed almonds, mix well and pour on to an oiled tray. Leave to cool. When cold, grind into fine pieces.
**2.** Beat the egg yolks, vanilla essence and 75 g/ 3 oz icing sugar until stiff. Mix in the finely ground almond praline.
**3.** Beat the egg whites and remaining icing sugar to a stiff meringue. Gently fold into the egg yolk mixture.
**4.** Fold in the whipped cream, taking care not to over-mix.
**5.** Pour the mixture into 12 ramekins or a 20-cm/8-in loaf tin, and place in the freezer for approximately 2 hours.
**6.** Before serving, decorate each parfait with a rosette of whipped cream and a chocolate ornament.
**7.** If made in the cake tin, turn out the frozen parfait, cut it into 2-cm/¾-in slices and place them on cold plates. Decorate as above and add a small amount of *sauce au kirsch*. Serve the rest of the sauce separately.

# Mousse au Yogourt Creole Sauce Caramel

*Yoghurt Mousse with Pineapple and Strawberries (or Kiwi Fruit) with a Caramel Sauce*

SERVES 8–10

*For the mousse*

| |
|---|
| 65 ml/2½ fl oz milk |
| 4 egg yolks |
| 25 g/1 oz vanilla sugar |
| 6 leaves of gelatine |
| 450 ml/¾ pt yoghurt |
| juice of 1 lemon |
| 4 egg whites |
| 75 g/3 oz sugar |
| approx 300 ml/½ pt double cream |

*For the fruits*

| |
|---|
| 1 fresh pineapple (or tinned) |
| 225 g/8 oz fresh strawberries (or frozen) or 2 kiwi fruits, sliced |

1. To prepare the mousse, bring the milk to the boil.
2. Cream the egg yolks and vanilla sugar well.
3. Gradually add the milk and mix well.
4. Return the mixture to the heat, stirring constantly until it starts to thicken (without actually boiling) and coats the back of a spatula. Remove from the heat.
5. Soak the gelatine in a little cold water, then stir it into the hot mixture until dissolved.
6. Add the yoghurt and lemon juice, whisk until smooth, then leave to cool.
7. Whip the egg whites stiffly and fold in the sugar. When the yoghurt mixture is cold, fold in the whipped cream and the stiff egg whites.
8. Pour the mixture into a large glass dish or 8–10 individual dishes and place in the fridge to set. (Depending on the strength/flavour of the yoghurt used, add more or less cream to suit individual tastes.)
9. To decorate the mousse, peel the pineapple and cut into thick rings (poach slightly if not ripe enough). Wash the strawberries and cut in half, then arrange the fruits on the set mousse and coat with some of the sauce just before serving. Serve the rest of the sauce separately.

*Caramel Sauce*

| |
|---|
| 200 g/7 oz sugar |
| juice and zest of 2 oranges |
| juice of 1 lemon |
| 75 g/3 oz apricot purée |
| 50–75 g/2–3 oz crème de cacao or Curaçao |

Melt the sugar over heat until it becomes a slightly dark caramel. Add the orange juice and zest, lemon juice and apricot purée. Mix well until all caramel is dissolved, then add the crème de cacao or Curaçao, and reheat the sauce a little.

# Gâteau Forêt Noir

*Black Forest Gâteau*

SERVES 10–12

*For the sponge*

| |
|---|
| 100 g/4 oz sugar |
| 4 large eggs |
| 20 g/¾ oz ground almonds, slightly roasted |
| 20 g/¾ oz ground hazelnuts, slightly roasted |
| 50 g/2 oz flour |
| 25 g/1 oz cocoa powder |
| pinch of cinnamon |
| 25 g/1 oz butter, melted |

### For the filling

| |
|---|
| 65 ml/2½ fl oz (approx) Swiss kirsch |
| 1 tin black cherries (Swiss) |
| 150 ml/¼ pt syrup/juice from cherries |
| 750 ml/1¼ pt fresh double cream |
| 25–50 g/1–2 oz vanilla sugar |
| 50–75 g/2–3 oz raspberry jam (preferably home-made) |
| 150–175 g/5–6 oz chocolate couverture shavings |
| 15 g/½ oz icing sugar |

**1.** To make the sponge, heat the sugar on a paper-lined tray in a 200°C/400°F/Gs Mark 6 oven. Turn down the heat to 190°C/375°F/Gas Mark 5.

**2.** Whisk the eggs at high speed for 1 minute, add the hot sugar and whisk to a firm foam.

**3.** Sieve together the slightly roasted almonds, hazelnuts, flour, cocoa powder and cinnamon.

**4.** Gently fold the sieved ingredients into the firm egg foam, then add the melted butter.

**5.** Spoon the mixture into a greased and floured sponge tin (approximately 22 cm/9 in across) and bake for about 25 minutes. When the cake is ready, turn it out and leave to cool.

**6.** To prepare the filling, mix the kirsch with the cherries and syrup, and set aside.

**7.** Whip the cream until thick, then add the vanilla sugar.

**8.** Cut the sponge into 3 layers. Soak the first layer with kirsch syrup, then spread with raspberry jam and 1 cm/½ in whipped cream.

**9.** Place half of the cherries on the cream and cover with the second layer of sponge. Soak the sponge with kirsch syrup then spread with cream and the rest of the cherries as before.

**10.** Cover with the third layer of sponge and soak this with the rest of the kirsch syrup.

**11.** Mask the top and sides of the gâteau with the rest of the whipped cream and cover with the chocolate shavings. Before serving, dust with icing sugar.

## *Vanilla Ice*

SERVES 12–16

| |
|---|
| 1.2 litres/2 pt milk |
| 600 ml/1 pt double cream |
| 1 vanilla pod or a few drops of vanilla essence (optional) |
| 10 egg yolks |
| 300 g/10 oz vanilla sugar |
| 65 g/2½ oz milk powder |

**1.** Bring the milk, cream and vanilla pod to the boil.

**2.** Cream the egg yolks and vanilla sugar well, adding the milk powder.

**3.** Gradually add the hot milk and cream to the egg yolks and mix well.

**4.** Return the complete mixture to the heat, stirring constantly until the mixture starts to thicken (without actually boiling). When it coats the back of the spatula it should be removed from the heat.

**5.** Allow to cool as quickly as possible, stirring occasionally – if vanilla essence is used it should be added at this stage. Strain through a fine sieve and freeze in a suitable container.

**For coffee ice** prepare a strong coffee flavouring with 5 tbsp water and 50 g/2 oz ground coffee or 25 g/1 oz instant coffee, and leave it to infuse for about 30 minutes. Add 40 g/1½ oz sugar, pass through a fine sieve, and add to the vanilla mixture.

**For chocolate ice** melt 150–175 g/5–6 oz plain couverture, then pour one-third of the hot vanilla mixture on to the melted couverture, stirring constantly until a smooth cream is obtained. Pass the cream through a fine sieve, and add to the rest of the vanilla mixture.

# Truffes au Rhum

### *Rum Truffles*

MAKES APPROX 1.2 KG/2½ LB TRUFFLES

| |
|---|
| 150 g/¼ pt double cream |
| 350 g/12 oz plain couverture (confectioners' chocolate), chopped |
| 2 tbsp rum, to taste |
| 50 g/2 oz butter, unsalted |
| 1.5 kg/3 lb tempered plain couverture (see below), for dipping |

**1.** Bring the cream to the boil in a double saucepan, and then leave to cool for 1 minute.
**2.** Add the chopped couverture and stir constantly over a moderate heat until melted.
**3.** Add the rum and mix well.
**4.** Add the butter and continue stirring to obtain a thick, smooth cream. Leave the pan to cool in iced water.
**5.** Pipe the mixture on to greaseproof paper in small mounds, the size of a large cherry.
**6.** Leave to harden, then roll in the hands into balls. Leave to set firm.
**7.** Hand-roll them with a little tempered couverture and replace on the paper. Leave to set.
**8.** Dip the set shapes in the tempered couverture and roll them over a fine wire mesh tray or sieve, to roughen them. Place on greaseproof paper and leave to set.

**For brandy truffles** substitute 300 g/10 oz milk couverture and 50 g/2 oz plain couverture, 2 tbsp brandy and 1.5 kg/3 lb tempered milk couverture for the plain couverture, rum and tempered plain couverture.

*Note:* To temper couverture, heat in a double saucepan to 49°C/120°F maximum, then cool to about 28°C/82°F by standing the pan in iced water and stirring constantly. Reheat to 31–32°C/88–89°F for plain couverture or 29–31°C/ 85–87°F for milk couverture, and maintain this temperature while dipping.

# Truffes au Cointreau

### *Orange Truffles*

MAKES APPROX 1.5 KG/3 LB TRUFFLES

| |
|---|
| juice and zest of 2 oranges |
| 25 g/1 oz sugar |
| 100 g/4 oz double cream |
| 100 g/4 oz plain couverture, chopped |
| 300 g/10 oz milk couverture, chopped |
| 2 tbsp cointreau |
| 50 g/2 oz candied orange peel |
| 50 g/2 oz unsalted butter |
| 1.75 kg/4 lb tempered milk couverture (see previous recipe), for dipping |
| cocoa powder |

**1.** Boil the orange juice, zest and sugar for about 2 minutes.
**2.** Bring the cream to the boil in a thick-bottomed pan. Leave for 1 minute.
**3.** Add the chopped couverture to the cream, and stir constantly over a moderate heat until the couverture has melted.
**4.** Then add the cooked orange juice and zest, cointreau and orange peel.
**5.** Continuing to stir, add the butter to obtain a thick, smooth cream.
**6.** Leave the mixture to cool, then pipe in small mounds on to greaseproof paper. Leave to harden, then shape into balls.
**7.** Roll the shapes in the hand with a little tempered milk couverture and replace on paper. Leave to set. (This thin coating gives the truffles the firmness needed.)
**8.** Dip the set shapes in the tempered couverture and roll in cocoa powder. Leave to set, remove from the cocoa and shake off surplus powder.

# Index